THE ORCHESTRA
AN INTRODUCTION TO THE WORLD OF CLASSICAL MUSIC

THE ORCHESTRA
AN INTRODUCTION TO THE WORLD OF CLASSICAL MUSIC

BY ALAN BLACKWOOD

A FIRST GUIDE
THE MILLBROOK PRESS
BROOKFIELD, CONNECTICUT

A QUARTO BOOK

First published in the United States of America in 1993 by
The Millbrook Press Inc.
2 Old New Milford Road
Brookfield, Connecticut 06804

Library of Congress Cataloging-in-Publication Data

Blackwood, Alan, 1932-
    The orchestra: an introduction to the world of
    classical music: / by Alan Blackwood.
       p.   cm.
    Includes index.
    Summary: Traces the history of the orchestra and discusses the
musical instruments that make up the various orchestral families.
    ISBN 1-56294-708-7 (trade ed.) 1-56294-202-6 (lib. ed.)
    1. Orchestra -- Juvenile literature. 2. Musical Instruments --
Juvenile literature [1. Orchestra. 2. Musical Instruments.)
    I. Title.
    ML1200.B54 1993   92-18412
    784.2 -- dc20   CIP
                                       AC MN

This book was designed and produced by
Quarto Publishing plc
The Old Brewery, 6 Blundell Street,
London N7 9BH

Creative Director Nick Buzzard
Editors Cynthia O'Brien, Louise Bostock
Designer Nicky Chapman
Illustrators Janos Marffy, Guy Smith, Danny McBride, Rob Shone
Photographer Phil Starling
Picture Research Liz Eddison

The Publishers would like to thank the following for their help in the
preparation of this book: Abigail Frost, Trish Going, Karen Ball

With special thanks to the London Symphony Orchestra and their Principal Conductor Michael Tilson Thomas

Typeset by En to En Typesetters, Tunbridge Wells, Kent
Manufactured in Hong Kong by Regent Publishing Services Ltd
Printed in China

CONTENTS

CHAPTER 1

INTRODUCTION

One of the most thrilling sounds is that of an orchestra tuning up before a concert. There is a buzz of excitement in the hall, as the audience take their seats and the players tune their instruments, running up and down a few practice scales, or trying out snatches of the music they will soon be playing. Then the conductor steps onto the podium, and there is an expectant hush. The baton is raised, and the musicians start to play, blending their sounds like one great musical instrument.

THE STORY OF THE ORCHESTRA

◄ Conductor and orchestra in action. The history of the orchestra goes back around four hundred years, but conductors became important only in the nineteenth century. Before that, orchestras were often directed by a violinist, or from a keyboard instrument, such as a harpsichord.

The word "orchestra" was first used nearly three thousand years ago by the ancient Greeks. It described the area of an open-air theater where dancing and singing took place during the performance of a play. Our use of the word, to describe a large group of instrumental musicians, is much more recent. Of course, musicians all over the world have been making music together for thousands of years. But the history of what we think of as the orchestra goes back only about four hundred years.

The connection between the two different meanings of "orchestra," the ancient Greek definition and our own, is an interesting one. Around the year 1600 — toward the end of the period of European history called the Renaissance — there was much interest among scholars and musicians, especially in Italy, in the drama of ancient Greece and how it was performed. This led to the creation of operas (plays set to music), which in turn led to the formation of the first groups of musicians — what we now call orchestras.

1607: Monteverdi's First Opera

The year 1607 is a key date in the early history of opera and the orchestra. In that year, the opera *Orfeo* was performed for the first time at the palace of the Duke of Mantua.

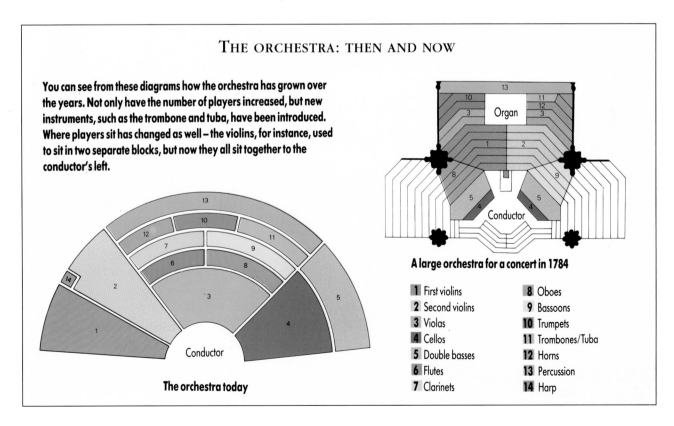

THE ORCHESTRA: THEN AND NOW

You can see from these diagrams how the orchestra has grown over the years. Not only have the number of players increased, but new instruments, such as the trombone and tuba, have been introduced. Where players sit has changed as well – the violins, for instance, used to sit in two separate blocks, but now they all sit together to the conductor's left.

Conductor

The orchestra today

Organ

Conductor

A large orchestra for a concert in 1784

1 First violins		**8** Oboes	
2 Second violins		**9** Bassoons	
3 Violas		**10** Trumpets	
4 Cellos		**11** Trombones/Tuba	
5 Double basses		**12** Horns	
6 Flutes		**13** Percussion	
7 Clarinets		**14** Harp	

It was based on an old Greek legend about Orpheus, who plays beautiful music on his lyre as a means of entering Hades (the Underworld) to search for his dead wife Eurydice. The Italian composer of this famous opera was Claudio Monteverdi (1567-1643).

In addition to all the music for the singers, Monteverdi wrote a good deal more for a large orchestra that included many of the best-known instruments of his time: two harpsichords; two or three small organs, or regals; a harp; a variety of stringed instruments, lutes, viols, and violins; woodwind recorders and cornets; trumpets and trombones. The piece he wrote for the start of the

▼ An early orchestra of string players performs at a theater. The strings were only one of the instrumental groups at the disposal of the composers of the time; in opera, masters of the orchestra like Monteverdi would have these groups playing independently as well as together, using strings alone, say, to characterize one character, and wind and organ to do the same for another.

MONTEVERDI: MASTER OF THE ORCHESTRA

The Italian composer Claudio Monteverdi (1567-1643) wrote vivid, colorful, expressive music that made the most of the orchestras of his time. He was one of the first composers to ask string players to use tremolo effects – literally, making shivering sounds – and to pluck their strings to play pizzicato. He was also a musical portrait painter; in one of his works, *Il Combattimento di Tancredi e Clorinda*, the story of a fight between two knights, his music depicts the sound of galloping horses and the clash of swords.

opera, with its lively and exciting rhythm, must have had the audience at the first performance on the edge of their seats. If we can single out one piece of music that really marked the birth of the orchestra, that was it.

From Opera House to Concert Hall

Opera, first in Italy, then elsewhere in Europe, quickly became the most popular entertainment of its day. Through the seventeenth and eighteenth centuries, hundreds of composers wrote thousands of operas, with singers and an orchestra, to meet the public demand. But orchestras were not confined to an opera house or theater for long. They were equally in demand to play in the palaces and other homes of the rich, and on ceremonial occasions. Many orchestras consisted of stringed instruments – the new violins, violas and cellos that were taking the place

▲ Monteverdi had his first pieces published when he was only 15. From 1590 to 1613, he worked at the court of the Duke of Mantua (left) and it was here that his first opera, *Orteo*, was performed in 1607. He left the city to take up a new post in Venice, which he held until his death.

ways of writing for these instruments, notably in a form called the concerto grosso, or great concerto. In such pieces, a large body of strings and a smaller group of soloists played in turn, creating contrasts of tone between them. Orchestral music like this went well with the grand and spacious style of architecture of the day.

The Earliest Concertos

One of the first masters of the concerto grosso and similar styles of baroque music was Arcangelo Corelli.

DID YOU KNOW?

about 42,000 operas have been written since its invention 400 years ago.

of the older types of viol. Violins, in particular, had a richer, brighter tone than viols, and could be played with greater agility.

Composers soon thought of new

▶ Musicians and singers gather together in this seventeenth-century painting. The musicians are playing viols, bowed, stringed instruments that were predecessors of today's violins, violas, and cellos. Viols had six strings, as opposed to the violin's four. They were also sometimes played differently, positioned upright and resting on or between the player's knees.

15

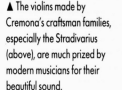

▶ Jean Baptiste Lully (1632–1687) moved from his home in Italy to France, where he became court composer to King Louis XIV, and made a fortune by staging his own operas. His tragic end was the result of his own quick temper; when beating time on the floor with his staff he wounded himself in the foot. The resulting infection led to his death.

Corelli and his famous contemporary Vivaldi were Italians, and most of this new orchestral stringed music was either composed in Italy or its style was copied by composers elsewhere. But in France there was another famous orchestra called Les Vingt-quatre Violons du Roi ("The King's Twenty-four Violins"). They belonged to the court of King Louis XIV, who built the magnificent Palace of Versailles, with its surrounding parks, lakes, and fountains, and they accompanied the elaborate ballets that the king so much enjoyed. His court composer, Jean-Baptiste Lully (1632-1687) and after him Jean-Philippe Rameau (1683-1764), wrote music for this kind of stringed orchestra, generally grand and stately, to match the elegant court or theater dancing.

CREMONA: BIRTHPLACE OF THE VIOLIN

Three families of craftsmen made the small Italian town of Cremona into the capital of world violin-making. They were the Amati family, the Guarneri family, and the Stradivari family. Andrea Amati established the basic design of the modern violin in the 1560s. The family business was continued by his descendants, including Niccolo Amati, who numbered Antonio Stradivari (right) and Andrea Guarneri among his apprentices. Both men went on to found their own violin-making dynasties.

▲ The violins made by Cremona's craftsman families, especially the Stradivarius (above), are much prized by modern musicians for their beautiful sound.

1 Antonio Stradivari
2 Carlo Bergonzi
3 Guiseppe Guarneri del Gesù
4 Antonio & Hieronymous Amati
5 Lorenzo Storoni & G. B. Ceruti
6 Francesco Pescaroli
7 Gio Maria Cironi
8 Niccolo Amati

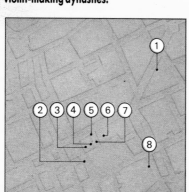

◀ Cremona was a small town in northern Italy. The workshops of many violin-makers, including the Amati, the Guarneri, and the Stradivari families, were huddled together in one district of the town, making this the center of the violin-making industry at the time.

▲ Antonio Stradivari (c.1644–1737) made at least 1,116 instruments during his long career, including 540 violins, 12 violas, and 50 cellos.

Cremona
•
Italy

Bach and Handel

Baroque orchestral music was by no means limited to stringed instruments. Toward the end of the baroque period, the German composer Johann Sebastian Bach (1685-1750) wrote his set of six *Brandenburg Concertos,* so named because he dedicated them to the local Margrave, or Prince, of Brandenburg. The concertos include parts for oboes, bassoons, horns, and trumpets. The trumpet is played in the "clarino" style, with an emphasis on very high, clear notes (see page 62). In Bach's day, good clarino trumpeters were popular and well paid. Bach also wrote some orchestral suites (groups of pieces based on old court dances). His famous *Air on the G String* comes from one of these.

George Frederic Handel (1685-1759) was also born in Germany. He traveled first to Italy, where he met Corelli, and then to England where he settled. There he wrote mainly operas and oratorios, but he also wrote very attractive orchestral music, including his famous *Music for the Royal Fireworks* and his *Water Music* for wind.

1700–1850: Classical Style

Orchestras of the baroque period could be large or small, with many different kinds of instruments or only a few. Much depended on how many musicians were available for a concert

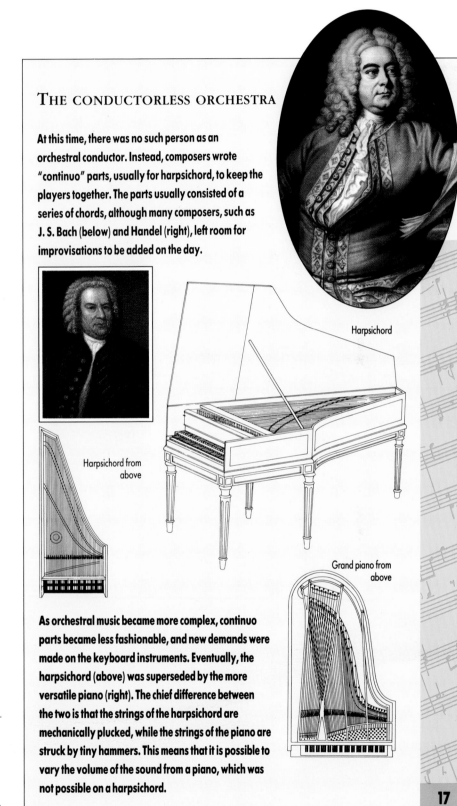

THE CONDUCTORLESS ORCHESTRA

At this time, there was no such person as an orchestral conductor. Instead, composers wrote "continuo" parts, usually for harpsichord, to keep the players together. The parts usually consisted of a series of chords, although many composers, such as J. S. Bach (below) and Handel (right), left room for improvisations to be added on the day.

Harpsichord

Harpsichord from above

Grand piano from above

As orchestral music became more complex, continuo parts became less fashionable, and new demands were made on the keyboard instruments. Eventually, the harpsichord (above) was superseded by the more versatile piano (right). The chief difference between the two is that the strings of the harpsichord are mechanically plucked, while the strings of the piano are struck by tiny hammers. This means that it is possible to vary the volume of the sound from a piano, which was not possible on a harpsichord.

▶ Haydn (1732–1809), pictured directing his classical orchestra from the harpsichord in a performance of an opera at the Esterhazy theatre.

or how many of them the person giving the concert could afford to pay. Composers themselves wrote for these orchestras in a generally polyphonic way – using a melody many times over, passing it from instrument to instrument, and weaving it around itself in sound.

All of this changed quite quickly around the middle of the eighteenth century. Styles in building, decoration, and design changed first. Many buildings were less grand than earlier ones. They were modeled more closely on those of classical Greece, with their orderly rows of columns and their pediments. The neat and elegant squares of Georgian London, Edinburgh, and Dublin, and many of the buildings of colonial America, are typical of this classical style.

This neat, elegant, and orderly style was soon echoed in music. The classical period in music covers the fifty years from about 1750 to 1800. Great changes took place in this short time, especially to do with orchestras and orchestral music.

New Music, New Orchestras

The style and form of much classical orchestral music was quite different from the earlier baroque styles. In place of the rich-sounding polyphonic music, with all the instruments adding to the melody, classical composers were more interested in the way music was put together, section by section, and the

The orchestra grew fast, so that it had changed enormously in little more than a century. Mozart's score for his *Jupiter* Symphony (No. 41) (below), written in the late eighteenth century, demands only a few instruments. The choice of these instruments depended on the players available at the time. For example, the *Jupiter* Symphony does not use clarinets, although Mozart often used them in other pieces.

By contrast, the score of Mahler's Sixth Symphony (right), written many years later, is much more complicated, and demands a far greater number of instruments.

Mozart

Mahler

In Mozart's time, most orchestral scores were written in Italian, and Mozart, although an Austrian, followed this style. However, a century later, Mahler, like many of his contemporaries in central Europe, preferred to use his native language, German.

way it should sound. From operatic overtures, or sinfonias, they got the idea of a composition with contrasting fast and slow sections. From the baroque suite they took the idea of a composition made up of several separate pieces or "movements." The main result of all these new aims and ideas was the orchestral symphony, a composition in several well-ordered and finely balanced movements – the musical counterpart, in fact, to one of those handsome classical buildings we have just been describing.

These classical symphonies, and other new forms of orchestral music, prompted changes in orchestras themselves. They were organized more like a team, with each group of instruments playing the parts best suited to them. The violins were best at playing melodies, with violas and cellos adding harmonies. Woodwind instruments, flutes, oboes, and bassoons, could take over from the strings and provide a contrast in tone. Horns, and sometimes trumpets and kettledrums, added their strong sound to moments of climax. Such a division of instruments into the four basic groups or "families" of strings, woodwind, brass, and percussion, became the foundation of the orchestra as we know it today.

An Army of Generals

In the latter part of the eighteenth century, classical-style orchestras, all organized in much the same way and playing much the same kind of music, sprang up all over Europe. They flourished especially in Germany, which was still divided into many kingdoms and principalities, each proud to have its own opera house and court orchestra. One of the best of these was in the Rhineland town of Mannheim, home of the local Elector, or Duke. He could afford the best musicians to play in his orchestra. The English scholar and traveler Dr. Charles Burney, on a visit to Mannheim, praised them as "an army of generals," meaning that every member of the orchestra was a first-rate player. Their skill and precision in playing together encouraged them to experiment with new orchestral effects, such as the crescendo, a gradual build-up of sound from soft to loud. This was a new and different effect at the time, which people spoke of admiringly as the "Mannheim steamroller." Some of the best classical composers went to Mannheim to direct the orchestra and write new symphonies and other pieces for them. One was Johann Stamitz (1717-1757), who arrived from Bohemia (now part of Czecho-

▼ For the Bachs, music was a family business: J. S. Bach's three sons all followed in his footsteps and became composers. Johann Christian (below), the youngest, settled in London in 1762, where he became music master to the royal family. When Mozart visited London as a boy, the two composers met and played music together.

slovakia), which was the breeding ground for many fine classical musicians. Johann Christian Cannabich (1731-1798) played in the orchestra under Stamitz's direction before directing it himself.

Another famous musical center was the court of the Prussian king, Frederick the Great, at Potsdam, near Berlin. Frederick played the flute and composed operas, symphonies, marches, and pieces for his favorite

▶ Frederick the Great was forbidden to play the flute by his father, who regarded music-making as an unworthy activity for a prince. As king, however, he not only played the instrument again, but even wrote concertos for it. In this painting, he is playing the flute in the music room of his palace at Potsdam. The accompanying musicians include C. P. E. Bach, seated at the harpsichord.

THE FIRST GREAT ORCHESTRA

In the eighteenth century, the city of Mannheim (below) was the home of the world's first virtuoso orchestra, funded by the city's proud Elector and packed with players especially recruited for their instrumental wizardry. Many composers of the time wrote especially for them, including Mozart, who lived in the city from 1777 to 1778. The orchestra also pioneered new musical effects, such as the crescendo, in which the sound gradually builds up from soft to loud – an effect that was described as the "Mannheim steamroller."

▲ The Elector of Mannheim, who put together the famous Mannheim Orchestra and employed influential composers such as Johann Stamitz (1717–1757) and Franz Xavier Richter (1709–1789). When the elector became King of Bavaria, many musicians followed his court to Munich, his new capital.

COMPOSERS ON TOUR

Many eighteenth-century composers worked for royal courts or aristocratic patrons. For twenty-nine years, for instance, Haydn's time was divided between Vienna and the summer home of Prince Esterhazy. It was only after his retirement that Haydn was free to travel, making two visits to London in 1791 and 1794. Mozart, on the other hand, was frequently on the move. As child prodigies, Mozart and his sister visited Vienna, Munich, Mannheim, Paris, London, Milan, Rome, Naples, and many other cities. In adulthood, concert tours and commissions often called him away from his home in Vienna, notably to Prague, where he scored one of his greatest successes with his opera *Don Giovanni.*

- 🔴 Towns and cities visited by Haydn
- ⚪ Towns and cities visited by Mozart
- 🔴⚪ Towns and cities visited by both Haydn and Mozart

instrument. He also employed one of J. S. Bach's sons, Carl Philipp Emanuel (1714-1788), who was a true pioneer composer in the new classical styles.

C. P. E. Bach's half-brother, Johann Christian Bach (1735-1782), worked in London, also writing sinfonias, concertos, and other new classical-style works. Both men looked upon their father as a very old-fashioned musician, which shows how quickly musical tastes and styles had changed in quite a short period of time.

Haydn and Mozart

Two composers, above all, brought the use and sound of the classical orchestra to perfection.

Franz-Joseph Haydn (1732-1809) directed the court orchestra of Prince Nicholas Esterhazy, whose estates were on the borders of Austria and Hungary. Haydn wrote dozens of symphonies, experimenting with better ways of writing for the orchestra. He decided that a symphony of four, well-contrasted movements — a fairly fast opening movement, a slow movement, a dancelike minuet, and a lively finale — was best. Many of these have nicknames because of some special feature in the music. Symphony No. 100 is "The Military." The size of most classical orchestras was around thirty-five players, but in Paris and London, Haydn was writing for larger ensembles than this. For his "Military" symphony, he added extra percussion and trumpet calls.

Wolfgang Amadeus Mozart (1756-1791) never had Haydn's luck. After fame as a child prodigy he had to work hard to earn money. But in writing symphonies he progressed, much like Haydn, from those that were similar to old operatic overtures to the last three symphonies (Nos. 39, 40, and 41, *The Jupiter*), which are models of the mature classical style, with their added depth of feeling and sometimes their grandeur. In his piano concertos, Mozart created a kind of "dialogue," or passing of musical ideas, back and forth between the soloist and orchestra. Beethoven and other later composers were clearly influenced by this new technique. Mozart was one of the first composers to include clarinet parts in his orchestral works.

18th–19th Century: Beethoven's Revolution

While Haydn and Mozart lived, America won its independence and became a new nation, with a president instead of a king. Soon after, in 1789, France also rose up against its kings. The new republic soon found itself at war with the rest of Europe.

These great changes were the background to the life of Ludwig van Beethoven (1770-1827). He brought the same revolutionary spirit to his music. He composed in classical forms, but the music itself has a new, sometimes wild sense of power and freedom. This is most evident in the way he wrote for the orchestra. The music often switches dramatically from soft to loud, from slow to fast. And at moments of climax,

BEETHOVEN THE REVOLUTIONARY

Ludwig van Beethoven (above) is universally recognized as one of the greatest composers of all time. His work bridged the classical and romantic eras in music. From 1801 onward, he was faced with increasing deafness; despite aids such as the ear trumpet (below), this gradually worsened until he became totally deaf in 1817. However, he went on to compose some of his finest works, such as the Ninth Symphony and the *Missa Solemnis*, in his Vienna studio (left).

ROMANTICISM AND THE GROWTH OF THE ORCHESTRA

The orchestra of Mozart's and Haydn's time consisted, on average, of forty-five players. By the time Beethoven was composing his last works, it had begun to swell, and by the end of the romantic period, it was enormous by comparison. The diagram here shows the number of instruments used by two composers, Beethoven and Richard Strauss, for pieces composed almost a hundred years apart.

Beethoven's orchestra for the performance of the Symphony No. 1 (1800).		Richard Strauss's orchestra for *Ein Heldenleben* (1898).
🎻🎻🎻🎻🎻🎻 🎻🎻🎻🎻🎻🎻	1st violins 2nd violins	🎻🎻🎻🎻🎻🎻 🎻🎻🎻🎻🎻🎻 🎻🎻🎻🎻 / 🎻🎻🎻🎻 🎻🎻🎻🎻🎻🎻 🎻🎻🎻🎻🎻🎻
🎻🎻🎻🎻	Violas	🎻🎻🎻🎻 🎻🎻🎻🎻🎻🎻
🎻🎻🎻🎻	Cellos	🎻🎻🎻🎻 🎻🎻🎻🎻 🎻🎻🎻🎻
🎻🎻	Double basses	🎻🎻🎻🎻🎻🎻 🎻🎻🎻🎻
	Piccolo	/
/ /	Flutes	/ / /
/ /	Oboes	/ / /
	Cor anglais	/
/ /	Clarinets	/ / /
	Bass clarinets	/
/ /	Bassoons	/ / /
	Double bassoon	/
🎺🎺	Horns	🎺🎺🎺🎺🎺🎺🎺🎺
/ /	Trumpets	/ / / / /
	Trombones	/ / /
	Tubas	🎺🎺
⚱⚱	Timpani (1 player)	⚱⚱
	Percussion (4 players)	🥁 🥁 △
	Harps	♪♪

Beethoven makes the trumpets blaze and kettledrums boom and roll.

His nine symphonies, especially, are like nine great stepping stones, leading orchestral music from the eighteenth century into the new, revolutionary nineteenth century. The orchestra Beethoven required to perform his Ninth Symphony was twice as large (seventy players or more) as that needed for the First Symphony. It not only had more of nearly everything, but included some new instruments as well. In this Ninth "Choral" Symphony, Beethoven added a large chorus of voices to sing his "Ode to Joy."

Romantic Music

Beethoven's *Pastoral* symphony (No. 6) is less dramatic and stormy than some of the others, but it was just as revolutionary. It conveys the passing scenes and moods of the countryside, describing in sound a gently flowing stream, birdcalls, a thunderstorm, and the sun coming out again from behind the clouds. No one before Beethoven had tried to make music paint such vivid sound pictures as in this symphony. It is an early and striking example of romantic music.

The word "romantic," as it is used here, has a much wider meaning than merely sentimental. It describes a whole period of art, literature, and music, belonging mainly to the nineteenth century. Back in the classical period of the eighteenth century, as we have read, composers took much care over the form and

Rossini: Master of Musical Excitement

In the overtures to many of his operas, the Italian composer Gioacchino Rossini (1792–1868, right) utilized to the full the musical possibilities of crescendo, getting his orchestra to play the same catchy phrase over and over, louder and louder. For this reason, he was known as "Signor Crescendo." Overtures such as *The Barber of Seville* and *William Tell* are sparkling pieces of orchestral music and concert favorites.

◀ The hairpin-like mark in the bass part of this score indicates the start of a crescendo.

▼ Composer-conductor Hector Berlioz made major new demands on the orchestras of his day as he conjured up exciting instrumental sounds to capture specific incidents, feelings, and emotions. Not everyone found this new music acceptable, as this cartoon of Berlioz in action on the conductor's podium shows.

style of their music. Romantic composers were more concerned with expressing their own thoughts and feelings through their music. They also wanted much of their music to evoke or describe a host of other things: poetry and legend; paintings; the beauties and wonders of nature; or the strange realms of magic and the supernatural, where they could really let their imaginations run free.

1830: A Fantastic Symphony

Nothing suited romantic composers better than the orchestra. For them, each instrument, or group of instruments, had its own special sound, suggesting particular moods or images. Horns, for example, suggested huntsmen and the open air. Clarinets evoked a mood of reverie or dreaminess. Tremolo violins and cellos (moving the bow rapidly to and fro across the strings) made a

▶ Felix Mendelssohn, one of the leading composers of the nineteenth-century romantic style. He is most well known for his concert overtures, which describe landscapes, events, and moods in pictures of sound.

MUSIC FOR A PURPOSE

Every major theater of this time had an orchestra – either to play "incidental music" to accompany a play, or simply to entertain the audience before the performance or in the intermissions between scenes and acts. Felix Mendelssohn (1809–1847) was just one of the many composers to work in this way with his incidental music for Shakespeare's *A Midsummer Night's Dream*. What makes this music unique is that the overture was written by Mendelssohn at the age of seventeen. The music for the rest of the play, including the magical scherzo and the triumphant "Wedding March," was composed many years later. Despite the time that had passed, Mendelssohn was able to recapture the mood that had inspired him as a boy.

◀ A scene from Shakespeare's *A Midsummer Night's Dream,* for which Mendelssohn wrote his famous incidental music.

DID YOU KNOW?

Beethoven's Symphony No. 9 was the first symphony ever to incorporate human voices.

shuddering sound intended to strike a tingle of fear in the listener.

Hector Berlioz (1803-1869) wrote a book on this type of orchestration — how to make the most effective use of instrumental sounds to conjure up feelings or images in the listener's mind. For him, the sounds of the instruments were like colors to a painter. He could blend them to make the orchestra come alive like a bright and brilliant painting in sound. Berlioz himself was a very "romantic" figure. As a penniless student in Paris, he fell madly in love with a young actress. This inspired his *Fantastic Symphony,* in which he evokes the dreams and nightmares of a young man half-crazy with love. It ends with a terrifying witches' dance. The *Fantastic Symphony* is miles from any symphony written before it, and it is a true sound painting.

Program Music

Other romantic composers wrote orchestral music as descriptive as that by Berlioz. In his opera *Der Freischütz* (about a young man who fires some magic silver bullets), Carl Maria von Weber (1786-1826) wrote spine-chilling music for the orchestra to highlight a scene filled with ghosts and demons. Felix Mendelssohn (1809-1847), when he was only seventeen years old, wrote an overture to Shakespeare's play, *A Midsummer Night's Dream*, capturing all its magic and fantasy. His overture, *The Hebrides* ("Fingal's Cave"), was inspired by a visit to the Western Isles of Scotland. The music suggests the sea swirling around the great rock columns that form the cave.

In *The Hebrides*, Mendelssohn was using the word "overture" in a new way. It is not an overture to an opera or a play, but a piece of descriptive music on its own. Franz Liszt (1811-1886) gave a name to the kind of

◀ The German composer Carl Maria von Weber (1786–1826) was a pioneer of descriptive, romantic music. He was especially fond of the horn, writing prominent parts for it in his opera, *Oberon*. He died shortly after conducting its first performance.

▼ Pianist-composer Franz Liszt, seen here playing for the Austrian Emperor Franz Joseph and his court in Vienna. Liszt invented the term "program music" to describe his attempts to tell a story in sound, and also wrote the world's first "symphonic poems."

TUBAS IN THE PIT

Wagner's operas or music-dramas are scored for a very large orchestra, sometimes with Wagner tubas, a type of brass instrument made to his own designs. He also built his own opera house at Bayreuth in Germany, totally concealing the orchestra from the audience and partly seating it under the stage (below left), so that its sound would blend in better with the voices of the singers and its presence would not detract from the stage action.

Richard Wagner (right, and in a cartoon, top) had pronounced views on how the works of composers should be interpreted and played. He even wrote a study of conducting, in which he said the main "task of the conductor was to give the right time to the band."

DID YOU KNOW?

Richard Wagner liked to wear fancy clothes while composing.

orchestral music that intends to create a kind of picture in sound, or to describe musically the mood of a poem or the events of a story: "program music." He coined another new word for some of his own orchestral compositions: "symphonic poems," which is a way of saying "poems in music." One of these is

Mazeppa, inspired by a poem by the British romantic poet Lord Byron, about a Cossack warrior who is captured and strapped naked to a charging horse. Another is *Hunnenschlacht* ("Battle of the Huns"), which describes in music a picture of a great battle.

Wagner and Music-Drama

Liszt's daughter Cosima married the composer Richard Wagner (1813-1882). But long before Liszt and Wagner were related through marriage, they were linked as two of the most daring and advanced composers of their time. They carried romantic music to new limits. In fact, Wagner soon left Liszt (and everybody else) behind, with his own fantastic ideas. He composed huge operas in which the drama and the music were forged together into one great work of art. For Wagner, the orchestra was as important, or more important, than the singing. He turned the orchestra into a marvelous tapestry of sound, highlighting every part of the drama as it unfolded on the stage. He even invented new instruments, such as the Wagner tuba, to achieve exactly the sound effects he wanted.

Wagner's greatest work is *The Ring of the Nibelungs.* It is made up of four linked operas, or "music-dramas," as he called them, inspired by ancient legends and myths about gods, dwarfs, giants, heroes and heroines, and a golden ring with a terrible curse upon it that destroys them all in

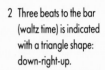
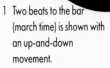

THE CONDUCTOR IN ACTION

Many textbooks have been written about how to conduct an orchestra, but most conductors have their own way of doing it. Some use very long batons, some very short ones, while others, such as the French composer-conductor Pierre Boulez, do not use a baton at all. Some make dramatic gestures and jump about on the podium, while others hardly seem to move, letting their hands and eyes do the work. Some read the full orchestra score, while others conduct from memory. Generally, however, conductors use the right hand (with or without a baton) to indicate to the orchestra the speed at which it should be playing. The left hand indicates expression, such as loudness and softness. You will often see a conductor raise a finger to the lips to emphasize that a passage should be played softly.

1 Two beats to the bar (march time) is shown with an up-and-down movement.

2 Three beats to the bar (waltz time) is indicated with a triangle shape: down-right-up.

3 When the music has four beats to the bar, the conductor makes a cross shape: down-left-right-up.

4 When the music has six beats and is played fast, the conductor may only beat twice, on the first and fourth beats of the bar. However, if the music is slow, the conductor may make a complicated triangle: down-left-left-right-right-up.

1

2

3

4

the end. The orchestral music of "The Ring" conjures up a whole world of images and actions: beautiful maidens swimming in the blue-green waters of the river Rhine; the clatter and clang of anvils in a metal foundry deep beneath the earth; a great storm and a rainbow bridge leading to a heavenly palace; magic fire surrounding a mountain top; and warrior-maidens riding across the sky on horseback (the famous "Ride of the Valkyries").

1876: Enter the Conductor

The first complete production of Wagner's "The Ring" — a truly colossal undertaking — was directed by Hans Richter in 1876. He was one of the first people to specialize in conducting orchestras.

Going back to the days of Bach and Handel, most composers, as we have read, played along with the orchestra, although in France there was a tradition for beating time on the floor with a heavy staff. When Lully (see page 16) was doing this one day, he accidentally hit his foot and died of the injury. Such methods of directing an orchestra began to change during Beethoven's lifetime. Orchestras were growing and the music being written for them,

DID YOU KNOW?

Leopold Stokowski conducted his first orchestra when he was only 12 years old.

▶ Brahms was so overawed by the legacy of Beethoven that it took him many years before he felt ready to compose his first symphony. This – and the other three symphonies he composed – are at the heart of the modern orchestral repertory.

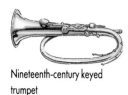

Nineteenth-century keyed trumpet

Modern valve trumpet

The design of most instruments evolved to meet the changing demands of musicians. The hunting horn was able to play only a few notes and was therefore used only to play fanfares. Over the years changes were made so that eventually it could produce all the notes of the scale, and play whole melodies.

especially Beethoven's, was more technically complex and demanded more expression and feeling from the players. In these circumstances someone was needed to take overall control of the proceedings, study the music, rehearse it with the orchestra, and direct or conduct the performance standing in front of the orchestra, where all the musicians could see him.

There are accounts of Beethoven himself trying to conduct, although they are very sad tales because he was going deaf and could not hear the orchestra properly. Weber, from all accounts, was far better at this new job of conducting. Another pioneer was the violinist François Habaneck in Paris, probably the first to conduct Beethoven's symphonies when they were still considered new and very difficult music. Mendelssohn, Berlioz, and Wagner were all good conductors, of their own and other composers' music.

So, with mention of Wagner, we come back to Richter, and to the beginnings of conducting as a specialist job. Since then, conductors have been among the most famous and glamorous figures in music.

Enter New Orchestras

Along with the introduction of conductors came big changes in the way orchestras were run. From the time of Monteverdi to Haydn and Mozart, most orchestras were privately owned by kings, princes, and other rich people. The Napoleonic Wars largely put an end to this aristocratic system. In the rapidly growing cities of industrial Europe and America a new type of orchestra took the place of the old court orchestras. These were like businesses, giving concerts in new halls.

One of the first of these new orchestras was the Leipzig Gewandhaus, named after the old "Gewandhaus," or Cloth Hall, where the orchestra originally gave its concerts. Mendelssohn was its musical director for some years. Many of today's other famous orchestras were founded during the nineteenth century: the Vienna and Berlin Philharmonics; the Royal Concertgebouw Orchestra of Amsterdam; the New York Philharmonic; the Boston Symphony; and the Chicago Symphony.

The Orchestra's Golden Age

As well as conductors and the new professional orchestras, the nineteenth century brought big

THE NEW AGE OF THE ORCHESTRA

By the nineteenth century, European musical life had changed beyond recognition. The performance of music was centered around specially built concert halls, played by world-famous professional orchestras and conducted by equally famous conductors. The Leipzig Gewandhaus Orchestra was based at a hall built by the city's linen merchants. Its first truly famous conductor was Felix Mendelssohn, who directed the orchestra for eight years between 1835 and 1843. Amsterdam's Royal Concertgebouw Orchestra played its first series of concerts in 1888 and was soon the national orchestra of Holland. Willem Mengelberg was its chief conductor for forty-three years, and it was under his direction that the orchestra began playing concerts in other European countries.

▲ This is the oldest known photograph of the members of the Gewandhaus Orchestra, taken in 1893. At that time, hardly any women played in professional orchestras, but one, the harpist, can be seen in the center of the picture.

▼ This advertisement is for the first concert ever given by the Concertgebouw Orchestra, under the baton of Henry Viotta. The orchestra numbered 120 players.

▲ Public concerts were held at Leipzig's new Gewandhaus, or Cloth Hall, from 1781. This picture shows a concert given in the 1840s by the resident orchestra. The hall had about eight hundred seats, and many of them faced inward (like choir stalls), which must have been very uncomfortable for the audience. The orchestra moved to a new, specially built hall in 1884.

Naamlooze Vennootschap
"HET CONCERTGEBOUW"
aan de Houbrakenstraat.
Feestelijke Inwijding
op 11 April 1888,
des avonds te half acht uur
GROOT VOCAAL EN INSTRUMENTAAL
CONCERT,
van de Heer Mr. HENRI VIOTTA de leiding
welwillend heeft op sich genomen.
SOLISTEN.
Mevrouw HARLACHER............ (Sopraan).
Mejuffr. CHR. VRIJMAN........ (Alt).
De Heer J. J. ROGMANS........ (Tenor).
"   "   Jos. M. MESSCHAERT... (Bas).
"   "   Jos. CRAMER......... (Violist).
Koor van 500 zangers en Orkest van 120 kunstenaars.

31

COMPOSERS WAVE THE FLAG

▶ Igor Stravinsky. Early in his composing career, Stravinsky favored using a super-orchestra, but, like Strauss, he later preferred smaller instrumental groups.

Some composers responded to the upsurge in nationalist feelings in the nineteenth century by writing music that reflected such emotions. One of the most famous pieces of nationalistic music is *My Country* by Bedrich Smetana (1824–1884). Smetana lived in Bohemia (then under Austrian rule, and now part of Czechoslovakia). *My Country* is a cycle of symphonic poems that pays tribute to the Czech national heritage.

◀ In Finland, Jean Sibelius (1865–1957) wrote *Finlandia* to express his country's desire for independence from Russsia.

▲ In Russia, Tchaikovsky (1840 –1893) composed his *1812 Overture* to reflect Russian national feeling.

▶ In England, Edward Elgar (1857–1934) wrote his *Pomp and Circumstance* marches as a celebration of the might of the British Empire.

▼ Elgar's *Pomp and Circumstance March* No. 1 features the tune that was later set as "Land of Hope and Glory." March and song are still performed at the last night of the Henry Wood Promenade Concerts in London.

improvements to the instruments, making them easier to play and giving them a generally smoother, sweeter tone. No wonder most composers of the time were fine orchestrators — skilled at bringing out the best in each instrument and setting the orchestra ablaze with sound. Johannes Brahms (1833-1897) and Antonin Dvořák (1841-1904) were fairly restrained in their orchestration, although they sometimes drew exciting or beautiful sounds from the orchestra. Others followed Berlioz and Wagner, making their orchestration one of the most striking aspects of their music. Listen to the way Russian composer Peter Tchaikovsky (1840-1893) makes the orchestra sing out the lovely melody in his fantasy-overture *Romeo and Juliet*, and how Nicholai Rimsky-Korsakov (1844-1908) creates dazzling sound pictures of stories from the "Arabian Nights," including the exciting story of Sinbad the Sailor, in *Scheherazade*.

Orchestras also grew larger and larger, with more strings, woodwind and brass, and many new instruments, mostly percussion: more types of drums, cymbals, gongs, xylophones, bells. Right at the end of the nineteenth century, Richard Strauss (1864-1949) included another extraordinary instrument, the wind machine, in his symphonic poem *Don Quixote* (see page 75), and both the wind machine and thunder machine in his *Alpine Symphony*.

In the early years of the twentieth

century, orchestras reached their largest size, with compositions being written for well over a hundred players. In Vienna, Gustav Mahler (1860-1911) – also a great conductor – recalled Beethoven by adding a huge choir to a gigantic orchestra in his Symphony No. 8, called *The Symphony of a Thousand*. In France, Claude Debussy (1862-1918) drew marvelously original sounds from a great orchestra in *La Mer*, a series of impressions of the sea, calm and sunny or in a raging storm. Maurice Ravel's (1875-1937) orchestral music for the ballet *Daphnis and Chloe* is famous for the episode within it that depicts sunrise – a great theme rising up on the strings, while the woodwind creates a rippling chorus of bird song.

The End of an Era

The famous ballet impresario Sergei Diaghilev asked Ravel to write the music for *Daphnis and Chloe*. He also asked Igor Stravinsky (1882-1971) to

As the nineteenth century drew to its close, the gigantic orchestra that Richard Wagner had created for his operas found its place in the concert hall. At the same time, composers wrote longer symphonies. The slow movement of Anton Bruckner's Eighth Symphony, for instance, is as long as a whole symphony by Mozart. Gustav Mahler's symphonies made similar demands, while the symphonic tone poems composed by the young Richard Strauss (1864–1949) called for some skilled playing – in one of them, *Don Quixote*, the orchestra had to imitate the bleating of sheep.

▲ Richard Strauss (1864–1949) followed Wagner in the use of the super-orchestra. However, in his later years, he moved away from using so many instruments. His *Four Last Songs*, almost the last music he ever wrote, were scored for a very small orchestra and a single, high voice.

◀ Part of the score of *Ein Heldenleben* by Richard Strauss, which requires a super-orchestra of more than 100 players. The more unusual instruments called for are the bass clarinet and the double bassoon, as well as a herd of eight horns.

write the music for another ballet, *The Rite of Spring*. This isn't springtime with apple blossoms and frisky lambs, but a cold, dark Russian spring, with the ice just beginning to crack and the first stirrings of life in the frozen earth. The ballet ends with a girl dancing herself to death as a sacrifice to the sun. At the first performance in Paris, in 1913, the audience was so upset they started shouting and fighting.

Stravinsky's music for *The Rite of Spring* marked the end of an era. He realized that there were limits to the

> **DID YOU KNOW?**
>
> the largest orchestra performed under Johann Strauss the Younger (1825–99), in 1872. It had almost 1,000 players (including 400 first violins).

▲ The American Aaron Copland (1900–1990) was influenced by jazz and traditional songs and music. He combined the two to portray life in the Wild West.

orchestra's size and the complexity of the music and that he had probably reached them. For the rest of his long life, Stravinsky experimented with different kinds of orchestras. In his *Symphony of Psalms*, for example, he omits violins but includes pianos.

Other composers of this century have turned away from the huge orchestra used by Richard Strauss, Mahler, and Stravinsky himself. In Finland, for instance, Jean Sibelius (1865-1957) sometimes wrote very sparingly for the orchestra, using only a few instruments at a time, to evoke the legends and the great forests and lakes of his homeland.

Sounds of America

While European composers were revising their ideas about orchestral music, American composers were writing for orchestras in other unusual ways.

Charles Ives (1874-1954) was brought up in a small New England town. He remembered the hearty hymn-singing and open-air parades of his childhood in many of his orchestral pieces. One of these is "Putnam's Camp," from a larger work called *Three Places in New England*. Various sections of the orchestra play different tunes at different rhythms and speeds, in the same way that Ives had heard two or three bands marching toward him from different directions when he was a boy.

George Gershwin (1898-1937) grew up in New York City and first earned his living playing the piano in "Tin Pan Alley," New York's old music-publishing district, where he learned about popular music. Soon

JAZZ MEETS THE CLASSICS

George Gershwin (1898–1937) combined jazz and orchestral styles in his famous "jazz concerto," *Rhapsody in Blue*. His other works include *An American in Paris*, and the opera, *Porgy and Bess*.

he was writing some of the best popular songs of the day, making him rich and famous. A bandleader, Paul Whiteman, asked him to write a "jazz concerto." The result was *Rhapsody in Blue*, a fresh and exhilarating piece that filled the orchestra with the rhythms and harmonies of jazz. In another jazz-inspired orchestral piece, *An American in Paris*, Gershwin daringly included parts for old Paris taxi horns.

Aaron Copland (1900-1990) turned for inspiration to the wide-open spaces of the American West. *Rodeo* is a colorful ballet about a cowboy get-together on a ranch, with the orchestra playing arrangements of old cowboy songs and dances. *Billy the Kid* is another ballet, based on the life of the old Wild West outlaw.

The Orchestra Today

Today some people say that orchestras are like musical dinosaurs – organizations that have outlived their time. The future, they argue, lies with electronic instruments, with tape recorders, synthesizers, and computers. Some of today's leading composers, such as Pierre Boulez and Karlheinz Stockhausen, have largely turned their backs on the orchestra as we know it. A group of composers known as minimalists have used tape recorders, electric organs, and synthesizers to produce "musical kaleidoscopes" – small (minimal) patterns of notes that keep changing by a few notes at a time. Orchestras play hardly any part in music like this.

But composers have continued to write original and imaginative orchestral music. The Soviet composers Sergei Prokofiev (1891-1953) and Dmitri Shostakovich (1906-1975) wrote great symphonies

MUSIC FOR MOVIES

The birth of the movie industry led to a new role for the orchestra. In the era of silent films, musicians on set provided "mood music" for the actors. When these movies were shown for the first time, full-size symphony orchestras played extracts from famous works, edited to accompany what was happening on the screen. Later, when it became possible to add sound to the pictures, film makers began to ask composers to write music especially for their films. The Russian composer Sergei Prokofiev (1891–1953) wrote several film scores, including the music to *Alexander Nevsky*. Musicals that had been successful on the stage were frequently transferred to film. One example was *West Side Story* (above right) with music by the young Leonard Bernstein (right).

▼ Prokofiev's score for *Alexander Nevsky*, keyed to individual picture frames.

and concertos. Prokofiev also wrote *Peter and the Wolf*, which introduces the many different sounds of orchestral instruments to young listeners.

Above all, more people than ever are going to concerts. For them, there is no substitute for the real thing: that thrilling sound of the orchestra tuning up to fill their ears with some of the world's most beautiful and exciting sounds.

DID YOU KNOW?

U.S. composer John Cage wrote a piece called *4 minutes, 33 seconds*, which is completely silent.

CHAPTER 2

THE INSTRUMENTS OF THE ORCHESTRA

A large orchestra is a magnificent sight, but it can also be a confusing one, with eighty or more musicians playing many different instruments. There are, however, only four basic groups or "families" of instruments. They may be classed scientifically as chordophones, aerophones, membranophones, and idiophones. But the groups are more commonly known as strings, woodwind, brass, and percussion. In the following pages each group of instruments will be shown in detail. A few composers have written pieces specially intended to highlight the different orchestral instruments in turn. Prokofiev's *Peter and the Wolf*, Britten's *The Young Person's Guide to the Orchestra*, and Bartók's *Concerto for Orchestra* do this brilliantly. There are many more famous pieces of orchestral music in which to listen for particular instruments. These pieces are listed in special boxes in each instrument section.

THE STRINGS

Many other stringed instruments, other than those of the orchestra, are played around the world. In an orchestra, the "string section" means the violins, violas, cellos, and double basses. They form a family, all looking very much alike, except in size, and all played in much the same way. In most orchestras they also make up the largest number of instruments, and have more to do than any other instrumental group or section, playing melodies and sounding harmonies. They provide a kind of cushion of sound for the rest of the instruments. Indeed, from the early days of the orchestra right up to the present day, composers have sometimes written music for a string orchestra, with no other instruments at all.

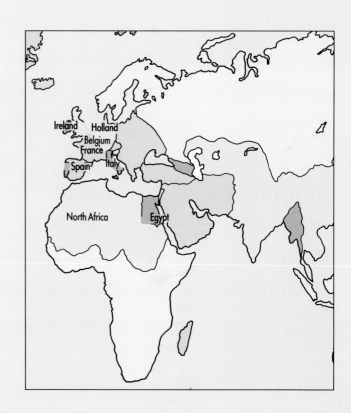

▶ The ancestors of almost all the string instruments used in the modern orchestra originated in Europe, North Africa, and the Middle East.

THE VIOLIN FAMILY

The violin family of string instruments descended from the rebab, an ancient instrument from the Middle East and North Africa. Like many Arab instruments, the rebab reached Europe when the Moors from North Africa invaded Spain, and when European soldiers went on the Crusades to the Holy Land (11th–13th centuries). The European version of the rebab was the rebec. Slowly, the rebec developed into the lira da braccio (the arm lyre), which had seven strings and two drone strings (strings that are not played, but which pick up the vibration of the other strings to produce a droning sound). The lira da braccio had a shape similar to the modern violin. In the 1550s, the first violins emerged in Italy. They had four strings and, like the lira da braccio, but unlike previous ancestors, violins were played resting on the shoulder.

Rebab   Rebec   Lira da braccio

◄ This ancient type of harp is known to have been in use in Egypt in about 1,200 BC. The musician would hold the thin neck of the instrument against his shoulder when playing.

► This Celtic harp dates from the 10th century AD. It has a roughly triangular frame and more strings that the Egyptian harp. The Celtic harp was probably supported on the knees and held against the chest.

◄ The modern harp is completely different to its two ancestors above. It is much larger, and has many more strings. It also has pedals, which change the length of the strings so that the harpist can play many different notes.

The first stringed instruments with keyboards, the virginals, the spinet, and the harpsichord appeared during the fifteenth century. These instruments produced a note by a mechanism that plucked the string when the keys were pressed. This plucking action meant that it was difficult to make the music louder or softer. However, in about 1710, Bartolommeo Cristofori, an Italian, invented a mechanism in which the strings of the instrument were struck by tiny hammers. This meant that the player could vary the volume of sounds. He called his instrument *gravicembalo col piano e forte* (the soft-loud harpsichord), from which we take the name piano.

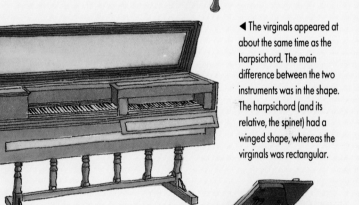

► Like all stringed keyboard instruments, the harpsichord consisted of a harp surrounded by a wooden frame. Its strings were adjusted to play all the notes in its range.

◄ The virginals appeared at about the same time as the harpsichord. The main difference between the two instruments was in the shape. The harpsichord (and its relative, the spinet) had a winged shape, whereas the virginals was rectangular.

► The grand piano, with its winged shape, is capable of producing a large sound, and is therefore good for use with an orchestra. The upright piano is small enough to fit into ordinary houses, and so has become very popular for home music-making.

Violin

39

HOW THE STRINGS WORK

▲ The kind of sound produced by twanging a rubber band depends on the tightness of the band and on the material it is made of.

Try a simple experiment. Take a rubber band or a length of string and stretch it until it is fairly tight. When you twang it, watch the band or string vibrate and listen to the sound it makes. Stretch it a little tighter and twang it again. It vibrates faster and produces a sound that is higher in pitch.

This is the acoustic principle of all stringed instruments. They have one or more strings, stretched across a frame, that are free to vibrate. How fast they vibrate has much to do with the pitch (the highness and lowness) of the notes they sound. Stretching the strings to different degrees of

CHANGING THE PITCH

The strings of some instruments are shortened when the musician holds them down with the fingers to produce different notes. The double bass player needs to hold down the strings at positions that are very wide apart, and so some teachers of the instrument recommend that double bass players practice with match boxes between their fingers.

tautness (making them tighter or slacker, as in our experiment) is one way of producing notes of different pitch. Another way is to use strings of varying length. A short string vibrates faster and sounds a higher note than a long one. Also, thin strings usually vibrate faster and produce higher notes than thick ones. Various materials have been used to make the strings of stringed instruments: strands of hemp and hair, silk, and the dried and stretched-out gut of an animal. Today, metal wire and nylon are most commonly used.

The strings of many instruments are twanged or plucked to make them vibrate. This is done either with the fingers or with a small piece of bone, ivory, wood, or metal, called a plectrum. Other strings are stroked with a bow. Playing a stringed instrument with a bow has a great advantage over plucking the strings. As long as the player keeps moving the bow across a string he or she can

EXPERIMENTS WITH STRINGS

Stretch a string across a box, and twang it to produce a note. If you change the tightness, thickness, or length of the string, the note will change.

Thin string – high sound
Thick string – low sound

Short string – high sound
Long string – low sound

Tight string – high sound
Loose string – low sound

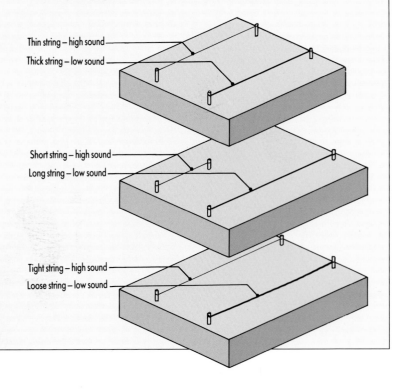

MAKING SOUNDS WITH STRINGS

Stringed instruments can be made to produce a note in three different ways. First, the string can be plucked, either with the finger, or with a small piece of horn or metal, called a plectrum. Second, the string can be bowed: The musician draws a bow made of horsehair or other material across the string to make it vibrate. Third, the string can be struck with a hammer. This is the basis of the mechanism of the piano.

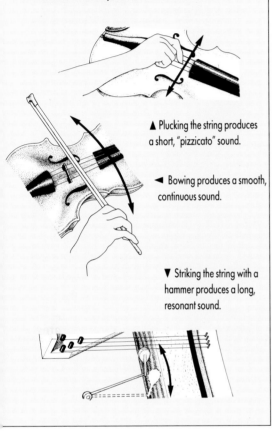

▲ Plucking the string produces a short, "pizzicato" sound.

◀ Bowing produces a smooth, continuous sound.

▼ Striking the string with a hammer produces a long, resonant sound.

resonator. It picks up the vibrations of the strings ("sympathizes" with them), giving them much more strength and character of tone. When we make a sound through our own vocal cords, our chest, throat, and head give strength and tone to the sounds in much the same way.

The frames or resonators of most stringed instruments are made from wood, which is an excellent material for the purpose, because it vibrates well. Some stringed instruments around the world also use gourds, the dried and hollowed-out husk or rind of a large fruit, as resonators. Painting or varnishing the wood or gourd can help too. Many stringed instruments are beautifully decorated in this way.

It is, of course, the construction of the frame or resonator, not the strings themselves, that has given us stringed instruments of such a wide variety of size and shape. It follows that an instrument with long thick strings and a correspondingly large resonating frame will produce deeper, richer-sounding notes than a much smaller instrument with thinner, shorter strings.

▲ The string is sounded and the vibrations spread through the bridge to the belly of the violin.

▲ From the violin's belly, the vibrations are passed to the back of the instrument by a post.

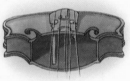

▲ They then spread to the whole body of the violin to produce a louder and more pleasing sound than the string alone could produce.

sustain the sound of a note. If a string is plucked (or hit), it soon stops vibrating and the sound dies away (decays) just as fast. Bowed stringed instruments can be plucked as well (called by the Italian word "pizzicato").

In fact, the strings on their own produce only a feeble sound, often not much louder or better in quality or tone than a piece of rubber band or string. For this reason, the frame of a stringed instrument has another important purpose other than simply stretching the strings. It acts as a

▼ The range and tone of notes made by a stringed instrument depend on the size of the resonator and the length and thickness of the strings. The small violin produces higher notes than those of the enormous double bass.

Violin   Viola   Cello   Double bass

VIOLIN AND VIOLA

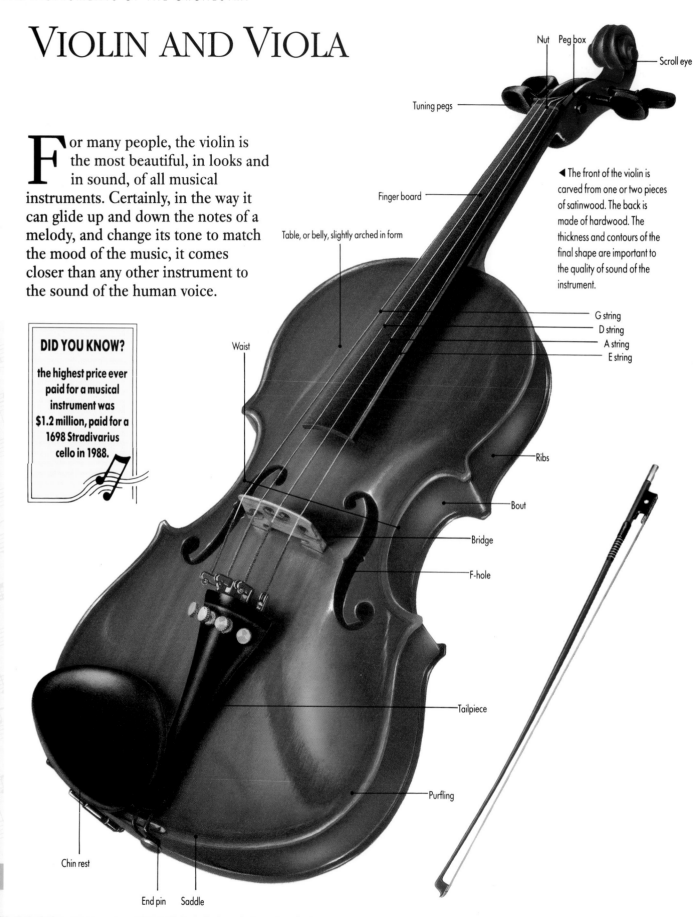

For many people, the violin is the most beautiful, in looks and in sound, of all musical instruments. Certainly, in the way it can glide up and down the notes of a melody, and change its tone to match the mood of the music, it comes closer than any other instrument to the sound of the human voice.

DID YOU KNOW?

the highest price ever paid for a musical instrument was $1.2 million, paid for a 1698 Stradivarius cello in 1988.

◀ The front of the violin is carved from one or two pieces of satinwood. The back is made of hardwood. The thickness and contours of the final shape are important to the quality of sound of the instrument.

Nut

Peg box

Scroll eye

Tuning pegs

Finger board

Table, or belly, slightly arched in form

Waist

G string
D string
A string
E string

Ribs

Bout

Bridge

F-hole

Tailpiece

Purfling

Chin rest

End pin   Saddle

The four full-length strings are known as "open" strings, each sounding its own note when stroked by the bow or plucked (pizzicato). The violinist sounds many more notes by pressing down on the strings with a finger (stopping), so shortening their playing length. Bowing technique is equally important. The player learns to draw the bow up and down across the strings, as a singer learns to take and hold a breath.

Almost from the beginning of orchestral music, violins formed the largest group of instruments, making up for their fairly quiet sound by weight of numbers, and also having the lion's share of the music. A modern orchestra may have up to thirty violins, divided into two sections: first and second violins.

The viola is only slightly larger than the violin, but this small difference in size is enough to give it a deeper range of pitched notes, and to give it a darker, or sadder, tone. Perhaps for this reason the viola has often been looked upon as a poor relation of the violin. Even so, many people love the viola. The great violinist Niccolo Paganini also owned a viola made by Stradivari, and asked Berlioz to write a piece for it. The result was *Harold in Italy*, which is a cross between symphony and concerto.

In the orchestra, composers often require the violas to provide a supporting harmonic line below the violins, although sometimes they give them a passage of music to play on their own.

STRING FACTS

Violin   **Viola**

Violin	Viola
80	30
70	
60	
50	15
40	
30	
20	
10	
cm	in

Length: 23.5 in (58 cm)   Length: 29 in (74 cm)

Normal pitch range: violin

G   C   G

Normal pitch range: viola

C   C   E

Location in the orchestra: Violins and violas

◄ Violinists and viola players hold the bow with their right hand. They use the left hand to support the instrument and "stop" the strings.

LISTEN FOR:

VIOLINS ··············

Mozart:
Piano Concerto No. 21 (second movement, playing the melody on muted strings, which softens their tone)

Beethoven:
Symphony No. 6 *Pastoral* (playing the main theme of the last movement)

Wagner:
The Prelude to the opera *Lohengrin*

Tchaikovsky:
Symphony No. 4 (third movement, playing pizzicato)

Holst:
The Planets ("Venus" and "Mercury," solo violin)

VIOLA ··············

Berlioz:
Symphony *Harold in Italy* (solo part throughout)

43

CELLO AND DOUBLE BASS

A large orchestra has a cello section of ten to fifteen players. They usually sit on the conductor's right-hand side, unless the second violins are placed in that position, in which case the cellos move closer to the center of the platform.

In orchestral music, the cello section often plays along with the violins and violas, adding splendidly to the rich sound of the strings as a whole. Sometimes, however, the cellos can be heard soaring away with a melody of their own. Occasionally, composers have written passages of music for solo cello (as part of an orchestral piece, not a concerto), or for just two or three of them.

Because of the rather deep, gruff sound of the double bass, and the fact that they are difficult to play at any great speed, the average six or seven double basses in the orchestra rarely have a chance to shine on their own. They are there to add depth and weight to the whole body of string sound. They also frequently play pizzicato, providing a very effective accompaniment to the rest of the orchestra.

Despite its fairly limited role, the double bass has had one or two star players: the Italian Domenico Dragonetti, who knew Haydn and Beethoven, and, more recently, the conductor Sergei Koussevitsky, who began his career as a double bass player and teacher. Both wrote music specially for this grandfather of the string section.

▶ The cello is about twice the size of the violin, with longer, thicker strings tuned to deeper notes. This gives the cello a stronger, richer tone than the violin.

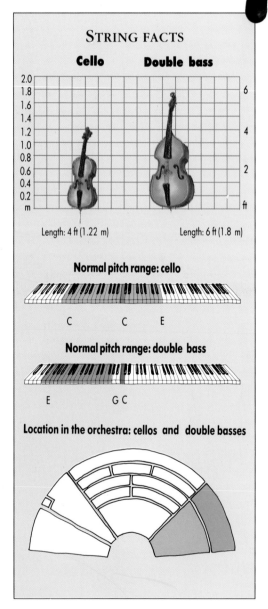

STRING FACTS

Cello   **Double bass**

Length: 4 ft (1.22 m)   Length: 6 ft (1.8 m)

Normal pitch range: cello

C   C   E

Normal pitch range: double bass

E   G C

Location in the orchestra: cellos and double basses

DID YOU KNOW?

the largest double bass ever constructed was 14ft (4.25m) tall and weighed 1301lb (590kg).

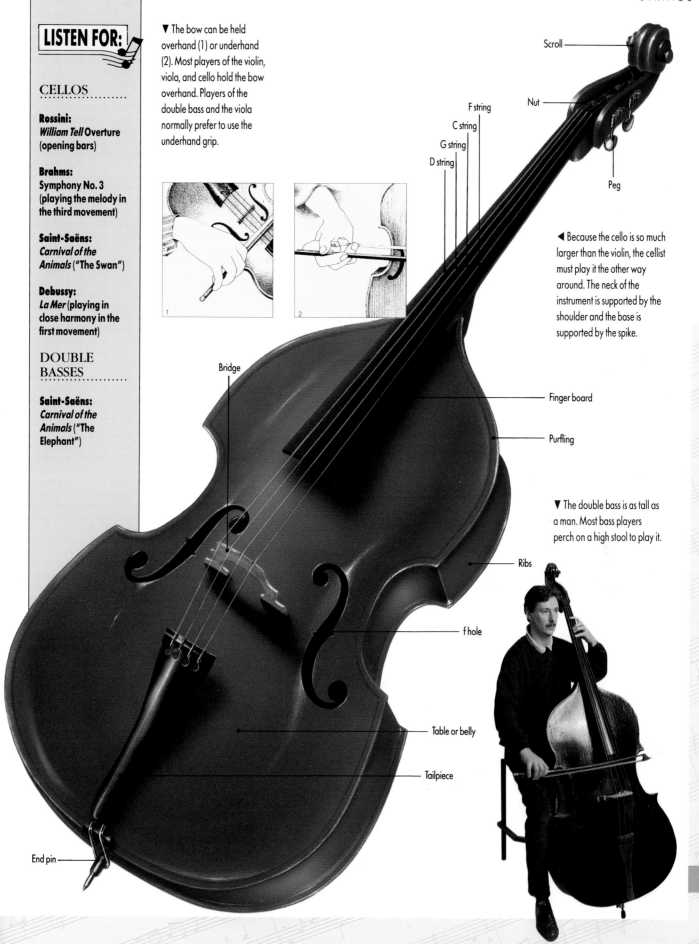

LISTEN FOR:

CELLOS

Rossini:
William Tell Overture
(opening bars)

Brahms:
Symphony No. 3
(playing the melody in
the third movement)

Saint-Saëns:
*Carnival of the
Animals* ("The Swan")

Debussy:
La Mer (playing in
close harmony in the
first movement)

DOUBLE BASSES

Saint-Saëns:
*Carnival of the
Animals* ("The
Elephant")

▼ The bow can be held
overhand (1) or underhand
(2). Most players of the violin,
viola, and cello hold the bow
overhand. Players of the
double bass and the viola
normally prefer to use the
underhand grip.

Scroll

Nut

F string

C string

G string

D string

Peg

◄ Because the cello is so much
larger than the violin, the cellist
must play it the other way
around. The neck of the
instrument is supported by the
shoulder and the base is
supported by the spike.

Finger board

Purfling

Bridge

▼ The double bass is as tall as
a man. Most bass players
perch on a high stool to play it.

Ribs

f hole

Table or belly

Tailpiece

End pin

45

HARP AND PIANO

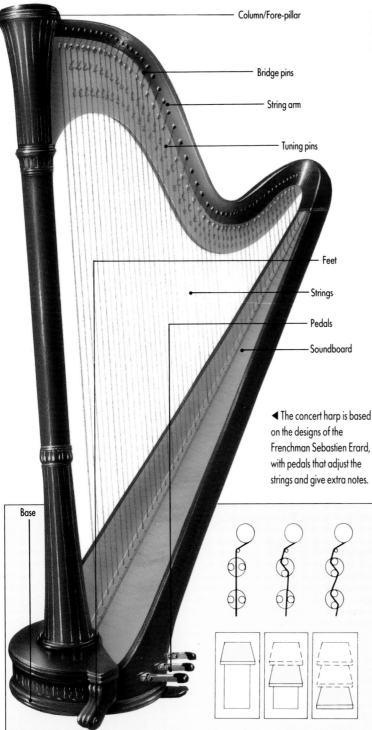

Column/Fore-pillar

Bridge pins

String arm

Tuning pins

Feet

Strings

Pedals

Soundboard

Base

▶ The harpist plays with both hands, using the thumb and first three fingers.

◀ The concert harp is based on the designs of the Frenchman Sebastien Erard, with pedals that adjust the strings and give extra notes.

T he harp is different from the violin and other bowed stringed instruments, being a plucked stringed instrument, with a string of different length and tension for each note.

Monteverdi included a harp in his orchestra for the first performance of the opera *Orfeo* in 1607. After that, the

DOUBLE-ACTION MECHANISM

If the harp had a string for every single note, either it would be a very big instrument or the strings would be too close together to pluck. The modern harp therefore has seven pedals, each connected to two disks. When a pedal is pressed halfway, the disk rotates, shortening the string and raising its pitch by a semitone. Press the pedal down all the way, and the disk rotates again to produce a note another semitone higher. In this way, each string can be made to sound three different notes.

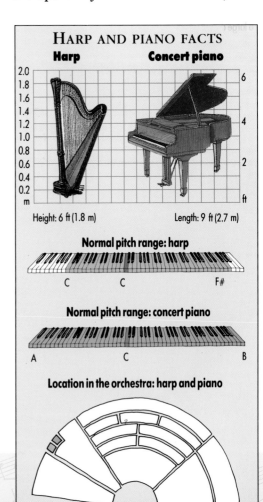

HARP AND PIANO FACTS
Harp   **Concert piano**

Height: 6 ft (1.8 m)   Length: 9 ft (2.7 m)

Normal pitch range: harp

C   C   F#

Normal pitch range: concert piano

A   C   B

Location in the orchestra: harp and piano

46

harp dropped out of orchestral music almost entirely for the next two hundred years.

Berlioz, one of the first masters of romantic orchestration, realized that the harp's delicate tones could sound well in an orchestra, especially playing runs of notes ("arpeggios"). The great orchestrators from that time on – Wagner, Tchaikovsky, Mahler, Debussy, Ravel, Elgar, and Stravinsky – frequently included a harp part in their scores.

The solo piano has inspired more great concertos than all other solo instruments put together. But it had to wait until the early years of this century to be included as an orchestral instrument, its percussive sound cutting through the smoother sound

of the other stringed instruments.

It is basically a harp laid on its side, encased in a wooden frame, with a keyboard attached. Hammers strike the strings and bounce off again, allowing a large dynamic range (softness and loudness). This mechanism was invented by the Italian Bartolomeo Cristofori in about 1710. He called his new instrument the "pianoforte" – the "soft-loud" – or the piano for short.

The little, tinkling celesta has tuned metal plates instead of strings, but it is played on a keyboard.

LISTEN FOR:

HARP

Berlioz:
Fantastic Symphony (second movement, "A Ball")

Holst:
The Planets ("Venus")

PIANO

Stravinsky:
Suite from the ballet *Petrushka*

Falla:
Ballet *El Amor Brujo* ("Love, the Magician")

▶ The grand piano. This picture shows a small, or "baby" grand. The total tension, or pull, of the strings of a large or "concert" grand piano, is the equivalent of about 30 tons in weight.

Keys

Strings

Pedals

DID YOU KNOW?

the world's most expensive piano was bought for $390,000 in 1980, by someone who could not play.

47

THE WOODWIND

Wind instruments of all kinds are classed as aerophones, that is, instruments that use air to produce their sounds. Many of these are woodwind. In the orchestra, the woodwinds range from the high-pitched piccolo to the very deep double bassoon or contrabassoon, with flute, oboe, bassoon, and clarinet all somewhere in between. Apart from their range of pitched notes, there are far greater differences in tone quality among these woodwind instruments than there are among the main section of stringed instruments, from violin to double bass. It is these tonal differences that composers like, often switching quickly from one woodwind instrument to another, to give their music variety and sparkle.

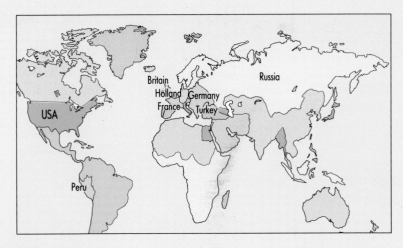

▲ Woodwind instruments of all types are used by peoples all over the world. Variations on the panpipe design have been found in places as far apart as China and Peru, and flutelike pipes are commonly used in the Middle East and Europe.

◄ The panpipes are an ancient form of flute, still used in many parts of the world today. They consist of a number of tubes tied together, each tube sounding a different note.

▶ This fipple flute is a forerunner of the modern recorder. It is thought that the first fipple flutes were being played in Europe during the twelfth century.

▲ This nineteenth-century fife comes from the United States, and was probably played in military bands. It is side-blown, like the modern flute, but its pitch is higher.

▲ The modern recorder is very similar to its ancestors. During the twentieth century the recorder has become a very popular instrument, especially for use in schools, and several modern composers have written music for the instrument.

▲ The modern flute is side-blown, like the fife, but instead of covering the holes with the fingers, the flautist uses a system of keys with which to cover them. Modern flutes are more likely to be made of metal rather than wood.

OBOES

CLARINETS

◄ A Turkish *zurna* (left) and a European shawm (below). Both are double-reed instruments, and both are ancestors of the modern oboe.

◄ Modern oboes were first made by the Hotteterre family, and appeared in France and England during the seventeenth century.

◄ This chalumeau, a precursor of the clarinet was made in the eighteenth century by Johann Christoph Denner in Nuremberg.

◄ The modern clarinet was developed in 1843, when the flute key system was adapted to suit the chalumeau.

◄ The bass clarinet plays an octave lower than the clarinet.

BASSOONS

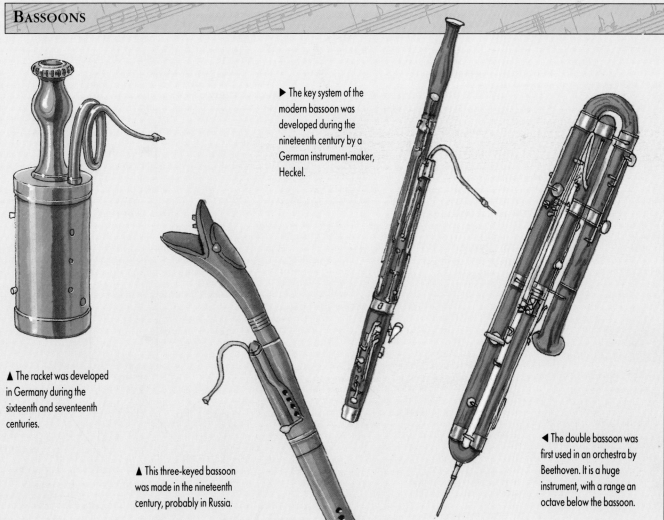

▶ The key system of the modern bassoon was developed during the nineteenth century by a German instrument-maker, Heckel.

▲ The racket was developed in Germany during the sixteenth and seventeenth centuries.

▲ This three-keyed bassoon was made in the nineteenth century, probably in Russia.

◄ The double bassoon was first used in an orchestra by Beethoven. It is a huge instrument, with a range an octave below the bassoon.

HOW WOODWIND INSTRUMENTS WORK

▲ When you put a blade of grass between cupped hands and produce a sound by blowing against it, you are making an instrument similar to an oboe or a clarinet.

Going back into history, woodwind almost always meant just that: wind instruments made from wood or cane. Today, some woodwind instruments of the orchestra are made from metal, and all have metal parts. This does not matter very much, because it is the way they are played that also classes them as "woodwind."

If you blow across the open end of a bottle, and get both the position of your lips and the amount of breath just right (don't blow too hard), you may start the air inside the bottle vibrating or pulsating. The resulting sound will be fairly soft and fuzzy. This is the acoustic principle of some woodwind instruments, like the flute.

Something else you can try is stretching a blade of grass between your cupped hands and blowing on it. With luck you'll get it to vibrate and produce another sort of sound, this time sharper in tone. This is the alternative principle of woodwind instruments, including the oboe and bassoon, that have a reed or reeds at their blowing end.

These principles, put very simply, are the ways in which woodwind instruments sound their notes. But that is only half the story. What happens to the vibrating column of air inside their pipe or tube is just as important. In a short tube, with a small diameter or bore, the air will vibrate or pulsate quickly and produce a high-pitched sound. In a longer tube, with a wider diameter or bore, the air will vibrate more slowly and produce a deeper-pitched sound. Compare the piccolo, with its short, narrow bore and very high notes, with

◀ Fill a milk bottle half full with water and blow across the top of it. Then empty out some of the water, and blow it again. You will find that the notes you are making are different pitches.

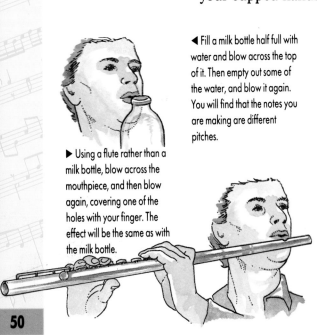

▶ Using a flute rather than a milk bottle, blow across the mouthpiece, and then blow again, covering one of the holes with your finger. The effect will be the same as with the milk bottle.

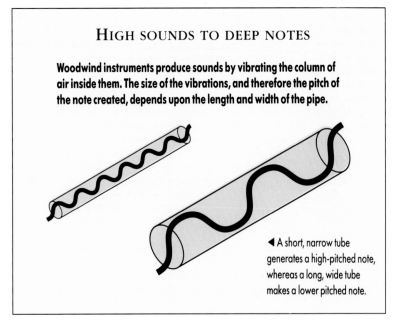

HIGH SOUNDS TO DEEP NOTES

Woodwind instruments produce sounds by vibrating the column of air inside them. The size of the vibrations, and therefore the pitch of the note created, depends upon the length and width of the pipe.

◀ A short, narrow tube generates a high-pitched note, whereas a long, wide tube makes a lower pitched note.

DIFFERENT WOODWIND SOUNDS

All woodwind instruments make sounds by vibrating a column of air inside them. However, each instrument makes a different sound from all the others. Most of the orchestral woodwind instruments have a more or less reedy sound. This is because the air is blown against a reed. The clarinet is one such reed instrument. The flute, however, has a smoother, gentler sound. This is because the air is vibrating against part of the body of the instrument itself.

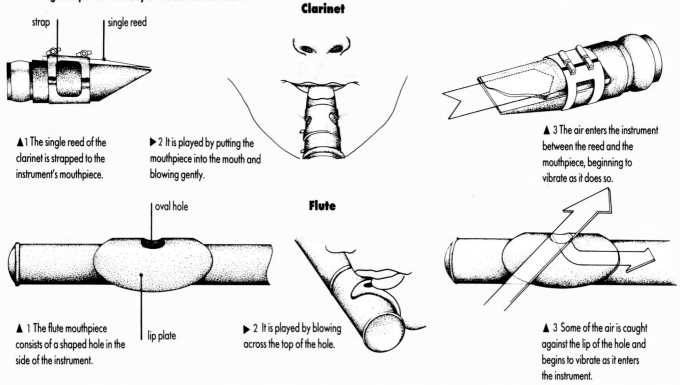

Clarinet

strap | single reed

▲1 The single reed of the clarinet is strapped to the instrument's mouthpiece.

▶ 2 It is played by putting the mouthpiece into the mouth and blowing gently.

▲ 3 The air enters the instrument between the reed and the mouthpiece, beginning to vibrate as it does so.

Flute

oval hole

▲ 1 The flute mouthpiece consists of a shaped hole in the side of the instrument.

lip plate

▶ 2 It is played by blowing across the top of the hole.

▲ 3 Some of the air is caught against the lip of the hole and begins to vibrate as it enters the instrument.

the long tube and much wider bore of the double bassoon, which sounds the deepest notes of all.

A few woodwind instruments, such as the ancient panpipes, have a pipe or tube of different length, and perhaps of different bore, for each note (as the harp has a string of different length or tension for each note). Most woodwind instruments, however, have a single tube with holes down the side. As the violinist stops a string to sound different notes, so the woodwind player covers or uncovers the holes to adjust the playing length of the tube (altering the length of the vibrating column of air inside the tube in order to produce notes of different pitch).

FOUR TYPES OF MOUTHPIECE

The clarinet has a single reed attached to the mouthpiece, whereas the oboe has a double reed. In the oboe, the two reeds vibrate against each other to produce a note. The fipple flute, or recorder, on the other hand, has no reed. The sound is produced by air vibrating against the fipple (the wedge of wood at the front of the instrument). The transverse flute has a hole across which the flautist blows.

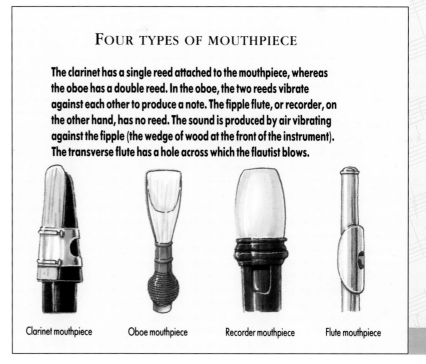

Clarinet mouthpiece   Oboe mouthpiece   Recorder mouthpiece   Flute mouthpiece

FLUTE AND PICCOLO

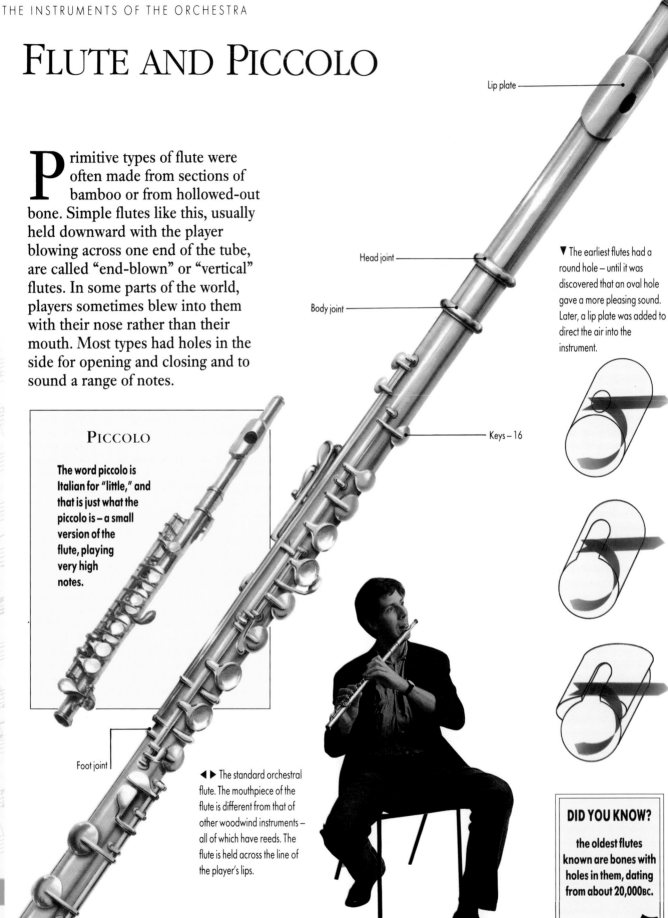

Lip plate

Primitive types of flute were often made from sections of bamboo or from hollowed-out bone. Simple flutes like this, usually held downward with the player blowing across one end of the tube, are called "end-blown" or "vertical" flutes. In some parts of the world, players sometimes blew into them with their nose rather than their mouth. Most types had holes in the side for opening and closing and to sound a range of notes.

Head joint

Body joint

▼ The earliest flutes had a round hole – until it was discovered that an oval hole gave a more pleasing sound. Later, a lip plate was added to direct the air into the instrument.

Keys – 16

PICCOLO

The word piccolo is Italian for "little," and that is just what the piccolo is – a small version of the flute, playing very high notes.

Foot joint

◄ ► The standard orchestral flute. The mouthpiece of the flute is different from that of other woodwind instruments – all of which have reeds. The flute is held across the line of the player's lips.

DID YOU KNOW?

the oldest flutes known are bones with holes in them, dating from about 20,000BC.

WOODWIND FACTS

Flute **Piccolo**

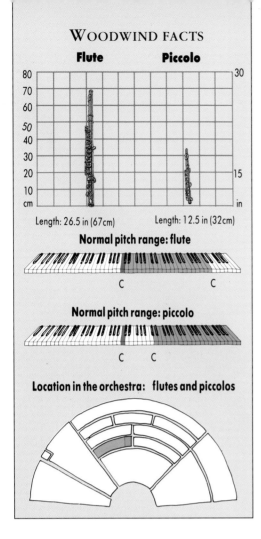

Length: 26.5 in (67 cm) Length: 12.5 in (32 cm)

Normal pitch range: flute

Normal pitch range: piccolo

Location in the orchestra: flutes and piccolos

The type of flute known best today, however, is the "side-blown" or "transverse" flute. The player blows across an extra hole (mouthpiece or "embouchure") in its side, and holds it horizontally (along the line of the lips). Early orchestral flutes of this type were still quite simple instruments, with seven or eight holes, which the flautist could open and close with fingers and thumb to sound different notes.

The eighteenth-century Prussian king Frederick the Great loved playing the flute, and it was his teacher and court musician Johann Quantz who designed a new type of instrument, with several levers, and pads to help the player cover and uncover the holes with greater ease and agility. But the real father of the modern concert flute was the nineteenth-century German court musician, Theobald Boehm. He re-designed the instrument with an entirely new arrangement of keys, levers, and pads, allowing for new combinations of covered and uncovered holes and a greater range of notes. Boehm also made some of the first all-metal flutes.

The modern orchestral or concert flute has not changed much from Boehm's design; and while some players may still prefer a wooden instrument because of its softer tone, most flutes today are all-metal ones. The well-known flautist James Galway has one made with gold.

The standard transverse concert flute (there are several different sizes, producing notes of higher or lower pitch) is larger than many people realize — roughly the same length as the clarinet or oboe. People also tend to think that the flute is highly pitched. But, except at the top end of its range of notes, it has a soft and mellow sound. Composers often write for it when they want to create a dreamy, romantic mood.

The piccolo is like the flute's little brother or sister. The name piccolo is short for the Italian *flauto piccolo* or "little flute." It is only about half the length of the standard concert flute, and it sounds notes an octave higher in pitch (eight notes higher) than the standard flute, making it the highest pitched of all orchestral wind instruments. Beethoven was one of the first to include it in his orchestral scores; you will hear it at the end of his *Egmont* overture, for instance. Since then, other composers have used its high, rather shrill tones to add an extra glint of color to the orchestral sound, a little like a painter adding touches of silver to a painting.

FLUTES

J. S. Bach:
Suite No. 2

Mendelssohn:
Overture and Scherzo from incidental music to *A Midsummer Night's Dream*

Debussy:
Prelude à l'Apres-midi d'un faune (the long opening melody)

PICCOLO

Beethoven:
Egmont overture

Tchaikovsky:
The Nutcracker Suite ("Chinese Dance")

Prokofiev:
Symphonic suite *Lieutenant Kije* (near the beginning)

OBOE AND BASSOON

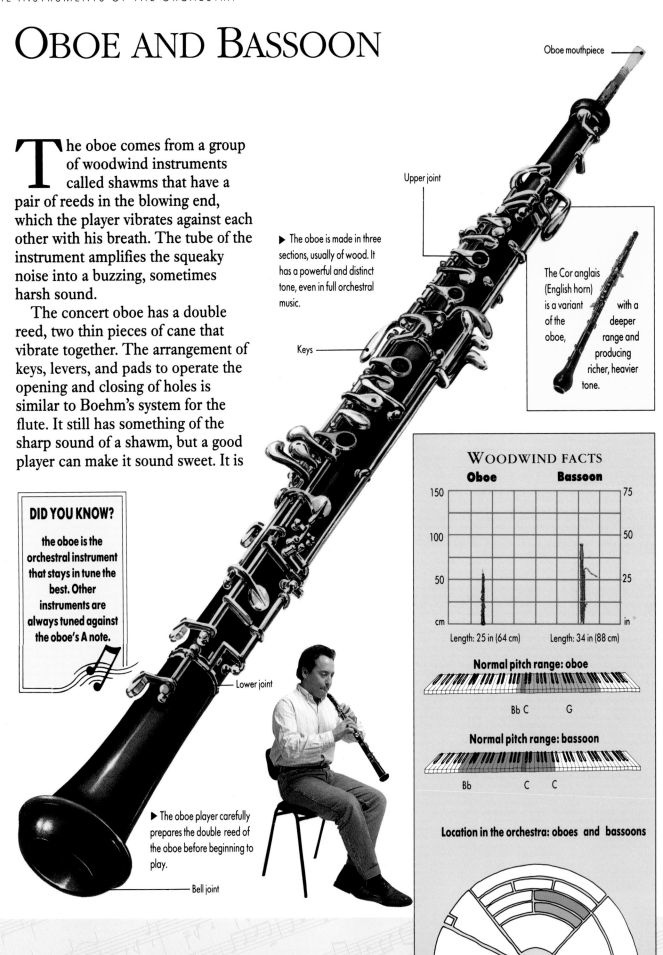

Oboe mouthpiece

Upper joint

The oboe comes from a group of woodwind instruments called shawms that have a pair of reeds in the blowing end, which the player vibrates against each other with his breath. The tube of the instrument amplifies the squeaky noise into a buzzing, sometimes harsh sound.

The concert oboe has a double reed, two thin pieces of cane that vibrate together. The arrangement of keys, levers, and pads to operate the opening and closing of holes is similar to Boehm's system for the flute. It still has something of the sharp sound of a shawm, but a good player can make it sound sweet. It is

▶ The oboe is made in three sections, usually of wood. It has a powerful and distinct tone, even in full orchestral music.

Keys

The Cor anglais (English horn) is a variant of the oboe, with a deeper range and producing richer, heavier tone.

DID YOU KNOW?

the oboe is the orchestral instrument that stays in tune the best. Other instruments are always tuned against the oboe's A note.

Lower joint

▶ The oboe player carefully prepares the double reed of the oboe before beginning to play.

Bell joint

WOODWIND FACTS

Oboe	Bassoon
150	75
100	50
50	25
cm	in

Length: 25 in (64 cm)   Length: 34 in (88 cm)

Normal pitch range: oboe

Bb C   G

Normal pitch range: bassoon

Bb   C   C

Location in the orchestra: oboes and bassoons

because of this clear tone that the oboe usually sounds a note A, by which the rest of the orchestra tune their instruments before a concert.

There are larger versions of the oboe. The oboe d'amore (oboe of love) was a favorite of J. S. Bach. The Cor anglais has a deep, rich tone, which appeals to many romantic composers.

The bassoon looks and sounds different from the oboe, despite its double reed. It has a conical tube (about eight feet long [2.5m]), bent double, producing the bassoon's distinctive tone. It has remained the standard bass instrument of the orchestral woodwind section for over three hundred years.

There are deeper versions of the bassoon. The double or contra bassoon has a tube that is about sixteen feet (4.8m) long and can go down an octave lower than the standard bassoon.

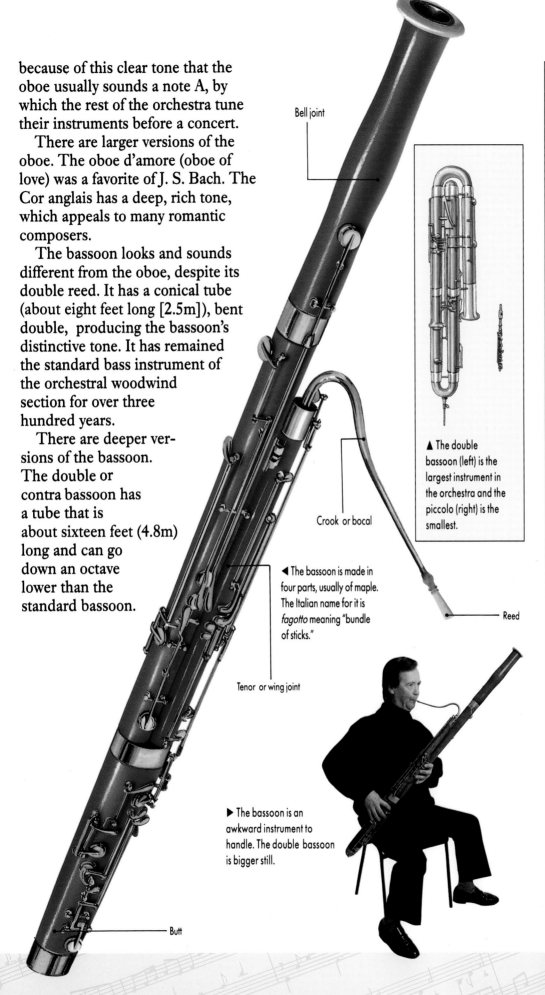

Bell joint

Crook or bocal

Reed

▲ The double bassoon (left) is the largest instrument in the orchestra and the piccolo (right) is the smallest.

◄ The bassoon is made in four parts, usually of maple. The Italian name for it is *fagotto* meaning "bundle of sticks."

Tenor or wing joint

▶ The bassoon is an awkward instrument to handle. The double bassoon is bigger still.

Butt

LISTEN FOR:

OBOE

Brahms:
Violin Concerto (opening melody in the second movement)

Haydn:
Symphony No. 88 ("trio") or middle section of third movement

COR ANGLAIS

Berlioz:
Roman Carnival Overture

Dvorak:
Symphony No. 9, "New World" (melody in the second movement)

Sibelius:
Symphonic legend, *The Swan of Tuonela*

BASSOONS

Tchaikovsky:
Symphony No. 5 (third movement, in waltz time)

Dukas:
Symphonic poem, *The Sorcerer's Apprentice*

Stravinsky:
Ballet, *The Rite of Spring* (the opening)

DOUBLE BASSOON

Ravel:
Suite, *Mother Goose* ("The Dance of Beauty and the Beast")

CLARINET

Mouthpiece ———

——— Barrel joint

——— Upper joint

——— Keys

Clarinets are a more recent addition to the woodwind section of the orchestra than flutes, oboes, and bassoons. They are descended from an older wind instrument called the chalumeau. Instead of the double reed of the oboe and bassoon, they have a single strip of cane inserted into a special mouthpiece.

Clarinets of various kinds (or "clarionets" as they were once called) date back to about 1700, but it was another hundred years or so before they became a regular part of the orchestra. Mozart was one of the first to include them regularly

▲ The clarinet reed is made of natural cane or fiberglass. The mouthpiece (known as its "beak") is usually made of ebonite or wood.

——— Lower joint

——— Bell joint

◀ The clarinet is the orchestra's most versatile woodwind instrument because it has a wide range.

LISTEN FOR:

CLARINETS
. . . .

Mozart:
Symphony No. 39 ("trio" or middle section of third movement)

Weber:
Der Freischütz overture

Sibelius:
Symphony No. 1 (opening of first movement)

Gershwin:
Rhapsody in Blue (opening bars)

BASS CLARINET
. . . .

Stravinsky:
Ballet, *The Rite of Spring* (opening section)

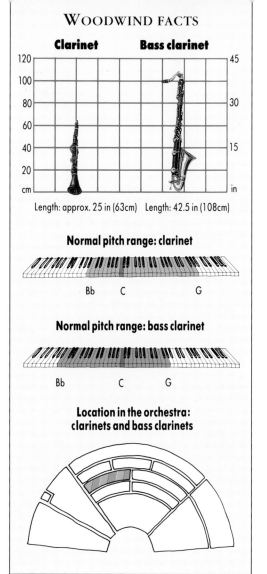

Clarinet   **Bass clarinet**

cm						in
120						
100						45
80						
60						30
40						15
20						

Length: approx. 25 in (63cm)   Length: 42.5 in (108cm)

Normal pitch range: clarinet

Bb   C   G

Normal pitch range: bass clarinet

Bb   C   G

**Location in the orchestra:
clarinets and bass clarinets**

in his orchestral music, although it was a deeper-toned version of the clarinet, the basset horn, that really interested him.

The modern clarinet has a system of keys and pads for covering and uncovering the holes, once again similar to Boehm's arrangement for the flute. It has a generally smooth and mellow tone, in comparison with the sharper sound of the oboe, which makes the clarinet ideal for taking orchestral solos.

There are several deeper-pitched versions of the standard clarinet. The bass clarinet, with its deep, full sound, is the best known. From about the time of Wagner, composers have included parts for it in orchestral pieces. The bass clarinet is not usually used as a solo instrument, but to add a dark, rich varnish to the woodwind sound.

▼ Clarinets use a single reed. Players can alter its position according to taste; they can also use harder or softer reeds, depending on their playing skills and the tone they want to produce.

Mouthpiece with reed

Crook

Keys (20–24 in number)

Bell pointing upward

THE SAXOPHONE

Around the year 1840, the Belgian instrument-maker Adolphe Sax invented the saxophone for use in military bands. The saxophone is made of brass, with a conical bore and a flared "bell," like other brass instruments. But it has a single reed inserted into a mouthpiece, like that of a clarinet, and holes in the tube, opened and closed by keys, levers, and pads, like other orchestral wind instruments.

During this century, the saxophone has been a favorite instrument among jazz and dance musicians. But some composers have also liked its creamy tone and written parts for it in their orchestral works. Listen for the saxophone in: Bizet's incidental music for *L'Arlesienne;* Ravel's orchestrated version of Mussorgsky's *Pictures at an Exhibition* ("The Old Castle"); and Prokofiev's *Lieutenant Kije* suite.

DID YOU KNOW?

Mozart is said to have liked playing billiards while composing music.

THE BRASS

Throughout history, trumpets have sounded commands of advance or retreat above the noise and confusion of battle, or they have accompanied pageants and parades. Huntsmen's horns have echoed through the forests and over the fields. People in Switzerland and Tibet have used giant trumpets or horns to call to each other across snowy valleys and icy mountain tops. These are the sounds of the great outdoors, piercing and strong. The brass section of the orchestra brings these sounds into the concert hall.

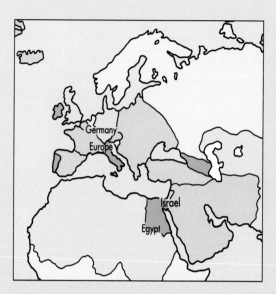

◀ People in many countries have used the forerunners of orchestral brass instruments. However, modern brass instrument designs originated in Europe.

HORNS

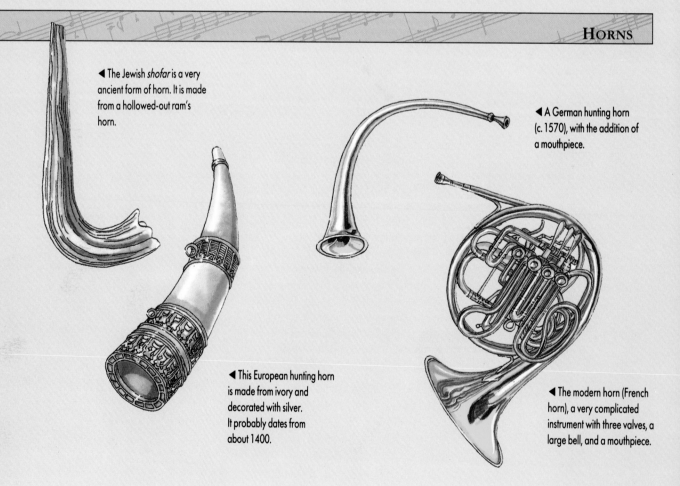

◀ The Jewish *shofar* is a very ancient form of horn. It is made from a hollowed-out ram's horn.

◀ A German hunting horn (c. 1570), with the addition of a mouthpiece.

◀ This European hunting horn is made from ivory and decorated with silver. It probably dates from about 1400.

◀ The modern horn (French horn), a very complicated instrument with three valves, a large bell, and a mouthpiece.

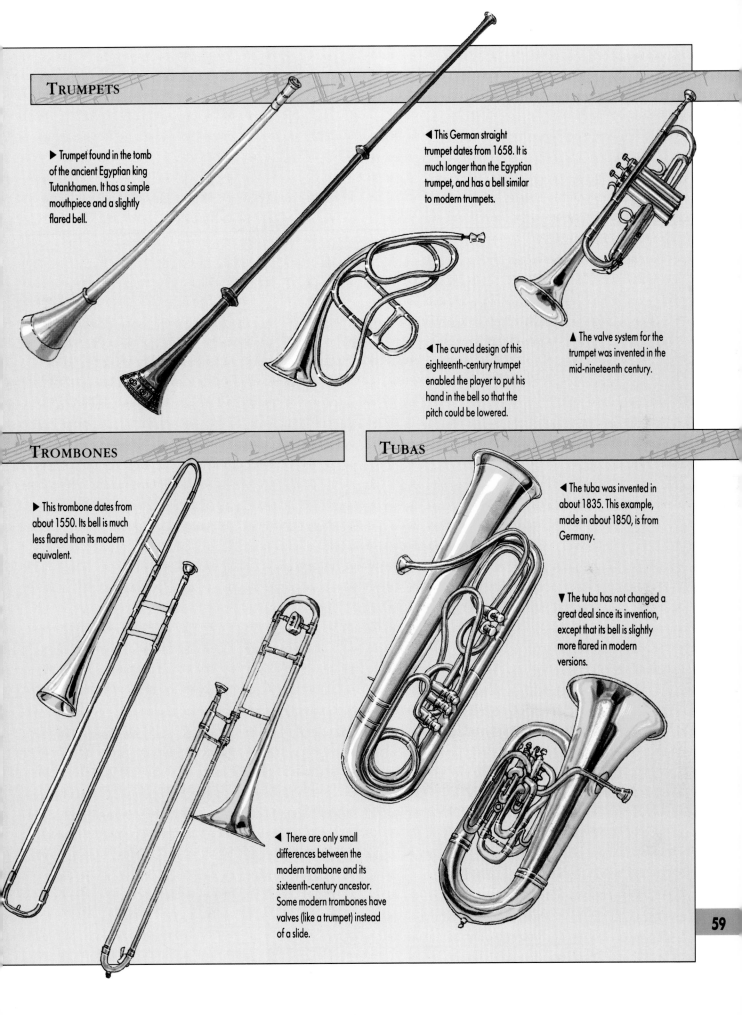

TRUMPETS

▶ Trumpet found in the tomb of the ancient Egyptian king Tutankhamen. It has a simple mouthpiece and a slightly flared bell.

◀ This German straight trumpet dates from 1658. It is much longer than the Egyptian trumpet, and has a bell similar to modern trumpets.

◀ The curved design of this eighteenth-century trumpet enabled the player to put his hand in the bell so that the pitch could be lowered.

▲ The valve system for the trumpet was invented in the mid-nineteenth century.

TROMBONES

▶ This trombone dates from about 1550. Its bell is much less flared than its modern equivalent.

◀ There are only small differences between the modern trombone and its sixteenth-century ancestor. Some modern trombones have valves (like a trumpet) instead of a slide.

TUBAS

◀ The tuba was invented in about 1835. This example, made in about 1850, is from Germany.

▼ The tuba has not changed a great deal since its invention, except that its bell is slightly more flared in modern versions.

HOW BRASS INSTRUMENTS WORK

▲ Take a piece of tubing or pipe. Put your lips together, press them against the end of the tuba, and blow hard. In this way you should create a note; the pitch depends on the length and width of the tube.

For thousands of years people have blown into hollowed-out animal horns or large sea-shells, producing loud, harsh sounds that can be heard over far greater distances than the sound of their own voices. They do it by pursing their lips tightly against the narrow end of the horn or seashell and blowing hard. This is a different process from that used for woodwind instruments. The player's own lips do the vibrating, and the air inside the horn, seashell or any other suitable object takes up these vibrations and amplifies them. You can create the same kind of sound by pursing your lips and blowing into a length of piping, even a length of stiff rubber or plastic tubing. This is the way all brass instruments are played, whether or not they are made from brass, another metal, or even another material entirely. The important principle of all such instruments is that the wider the bore of the pipe or tube, the deeper the pitch of the notes it will sound.

Up until about two hundred years ago, brass instruments nearly all consisted of one long tube, either straight or coiled around itself to make it easier to hold. They had a type of mouthpiece, or embouchure, at one end, into which the player fitted his lips, while the other end almost always widened into a flared bell to give strength and tone to the sound. Such brass instruments, with nothing added to the basic shape and size of the tube, are called "natural"

instruments. On these instruments a player can only sound a limited number of notes of different pitch (in technical terms, the principal notes of their harmonic series). He does this by pursing his lips more tightly or loosely and altering the pressure of his breath. This changes the pulse of the vibrations inside the tube. Old military trumpet or bugle calls were played on natural instruments, which is why they consist of only three or four notes.

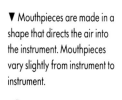

▼ Mouthpieces are made in a shape that directs the air into the instrument. Mouthpieces vary slightly from instrument to instrument.

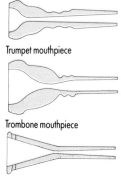

Trumpet mouthpiece

Trombone mouthpiece

Horn mouthpiece

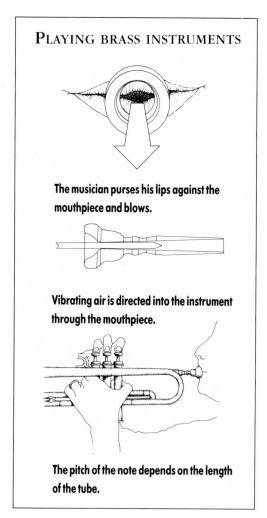

PLAYING BRASS INSTRUMENTS

The musician purses his lips against the mouthpiece and blows.

Vibrating air is directed into the instrument through the mouthpiece.

The pitch of the note depends on the length of the tube.

60

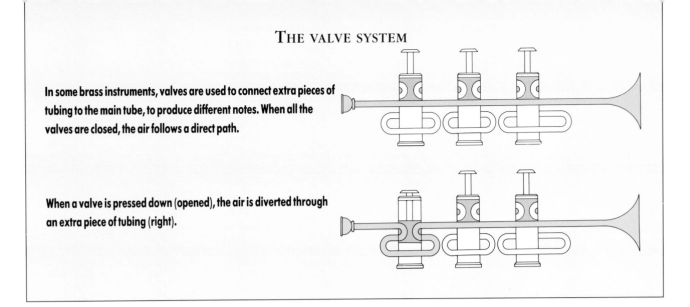

In some brass instruments, valves are used to connect extra pieces of tubing to the main tube, to produce different notes. When all the valves are closed, the air follows a direct path.

When a valve is pressed down (opened), the air is diverted through an extra piece of tubing (right).

Back in the seventeenth and eighteenth centuries, instrument-makers tried to improve on these instruments by making trumpets and horns with spare lengths of tubing ("crooks"). These could be inserted into the instrument to increase its playing length and change the pitch of the notes. This still had its limitations, since inserting a crook into the instrument only altered its basic tuning and did not really increase the number of notes it could sound at any one time (a bit like switching a train from one set of tracks to another).

Much more effective was the invention, around 1830, of piston valves. By pressing down or releasing these valves with the fingers, a player could instantly cut off or add sections of tube to the instrument's playing length. This allowed a much greater range of notes.

In modern brass instruments, the design of the mouthpiece is important too, helping to shape the player's lips in the way best suited to the instrument's pitch and tone. Brass players sometimes use mutes (metal, wooden or plastic plugs), which they insert into the instrument's bell to soften its sound, and sometimes to alter its pitch.

▶ Mutes (top) are used to reduce the volume of the sound made by a brass instrument or to produce novel sounds. They are placed inside the bell of the instrument (above). Horn players put a fist into the bell to produce a vibrant sound (right).

61

TRUMPET AND HORN

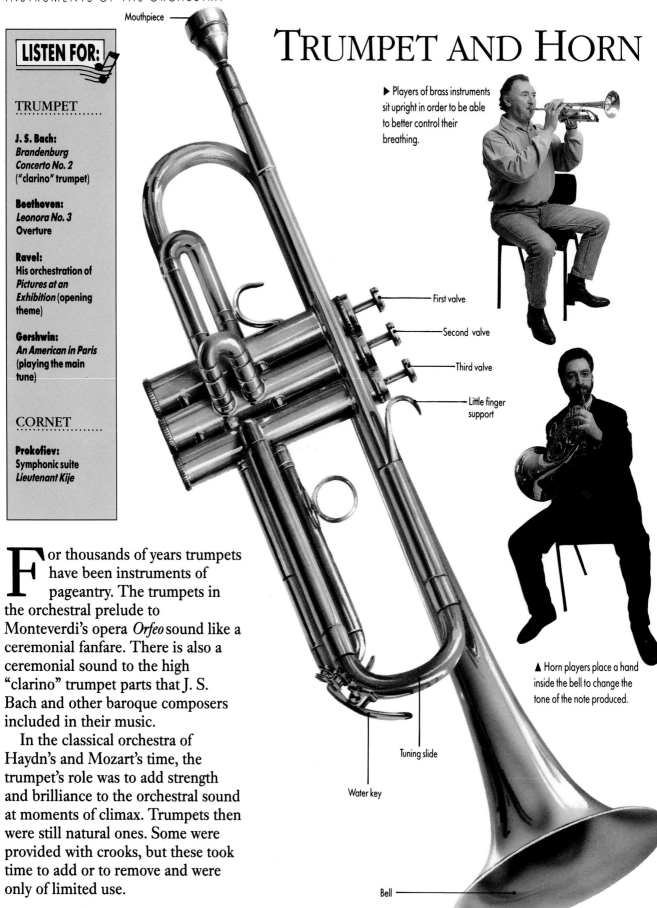

Mouthpiece

LISTEN FOR:

TRUMPET

J. S. Bach:
Brandenburg Concerto No. 2 ("clarino" trumpet)

Beethoven:
Leonora No. 3 Overture

Ravel:
His orchestration of *Pictures at an Exhibition* (opening theme)

Gershwin:
An American in Paris (playing the main tune)

CORNET

Prokofiev:
Symphonic suite *Lieutenant Kije*

▶ Players of brass instruments sit upright in order to be able to better control their breathing.

First valve

Second valve

Third valve

Little finger support

▲ Horn players place a hand inside the bell to change the tone of the note produced.

Water key

Tuning slide

Bell

F or thousands of years trumpets have been instruments of pageantry. The trumpets in the orchestral prelude to Monteverdi's opera *Orfeo* sound like a ceremonial fanfare. There is also a ceremonial sound to the high "clarino" trumpet parts that J. S. Bach and other baroque composers included in their music.

In the classical orchestra of Haydn's and Mozart's time, the trumpet's role was to add strength and brilliance to the orchestral sound at moments of climax. Trumpets then were still natural ones. Some were provided with crooks, but these took time to add or to remove and were only of limited use.

Mouthpiece

Brace

Crook

First valve

Second valve

Third valve

Bell

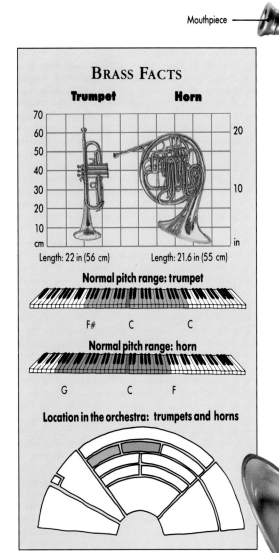

BRASS FACTS

Trumpet	Horn

70
60
50
40
30
20
10
cm

20

10

in

Length: 22 in (56 cm)

Length: 21.6 in (55 cm)

Normal pitch range: trumpet

F#   C   C

Normal pitch range: horn

G   C   F

Location in the orchestra: trumpets and horns

Valves made a great difference. From the time of Berlioz, composers wrote more elaborate trumpet parts, allowing the bright, sometimes piercing tones to ride high above the rest of the orchestra. The cornet, like a trumpet with a deeper tone, is sometimes used as well.

Like the trumpet, the natural horn had a limited range and many were supplied with crooks. In the case of the horn, the player could also place a hand inside the large bell of the instrument, which acted as a mute and altered the pitch of the note. The addition of valves in the early part of the nineteenth century gave the horn a greater flexibility and a wider range of notes.

◀ The horn was developed from the old hunting horns favored by the kings of France.

DID YOU KNOW?

that when King George III of England first heard the Hallelujah chorus from *Messiah*, he motioned the entire audience to stand — a practice that is followed to this day.

LISTEN FOR:

HORN(S)

Beethoven:
Symphony No. 3, *Eroica* ("trio," or middle section of third movement)

Weber:
Der Freischütz overture (opening bars)

Schumann:
Konzertstück (Concert Piece) for four horns

Richard Strauss:
Symphonic poem *Till Eulenspiegel*

Britten:
Serenade for Tenor, Horn and Strings (the composer asks for an old "natural" horn to be played)

TROMBONE AND TUBA

The trombone has a slide valve mechanism, which sets it apart from all the other brass instruments. This lengthens or shortens the instrument's playing length and produces a wide range of notes. It also allows a "glissando" effect, sliding up and down the scale from one note to another.

Trombones date from the fifteenth century, when new skills in metalwork brought improvements to brass instruments as a whole.

The tone of the trombone is generally richer than that of the trumpet, and can sound grand or solemn. In Renaissance and baroque times it was often used for ceremonial occasions. Mozart was one of the first composers to include trombones in the classical orchestra (in an opera), and Beethoven included them in his Fifth Symphony. But it was only during the nineteenth century that trombones became regular members of the brass section. The trombone section of the orchestra often consists of two tenor and one bass trombone.

Compensating weight to help balance the instrument in its playing position.

Mouthpiece

▲ The trombonist can operate the slide valve in seven different positions.

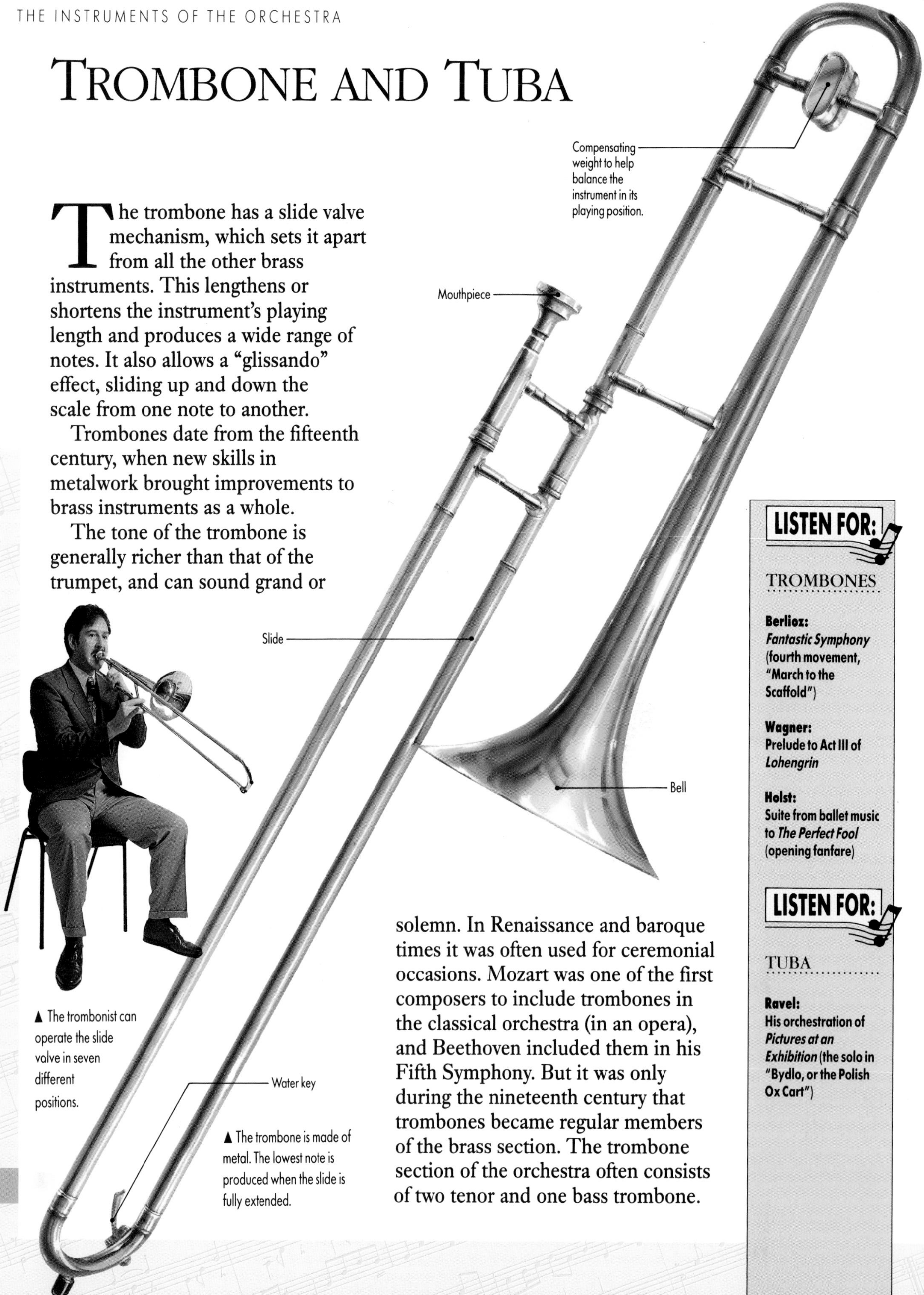

Slide

Water key

▲ The trombone is made of metal. The lowest note is produced when the slide is fully extended.

Bell

LISTEN FOR:

TROMBONES

Berlioz:
Fantastic Symphony (fourth movement, "March to the Scaffold")

Wagner:
Prelude to Act III of *Lohengrin*

Holst:
Suite from ballet music to *The Perfect Fool* (opening fanfare)

LISTEN FOR:

TUBA

Ravel:
His orchestration of *Pictures at an Exhibition* (the solo in "Bydlo, or the Polish Ox Cart")

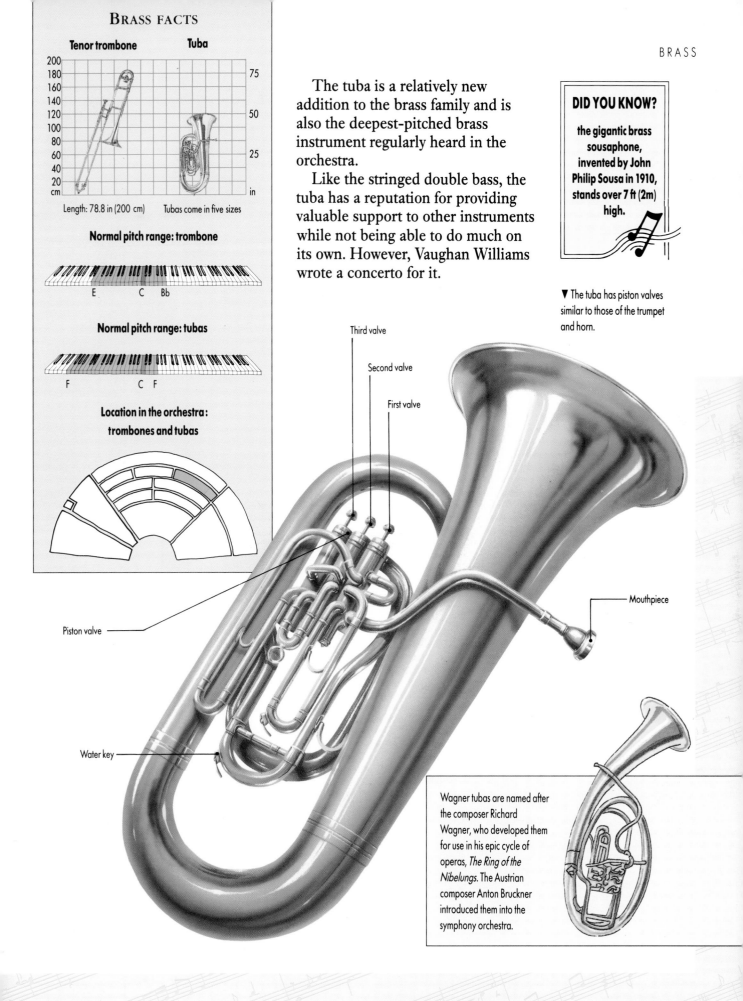

BRASS FACTS

Tenor trombone   **Tuba**

cm		in
200		
180		75
160		
140		
120		50
100		
80		
60		25
40		
20		
cm		in

Length: 78.8 in (200 cm)   Tubas come in five sizes

Normal pitch range: trombone

E   C   Bb

Normal pitch range: tubas

F   C   F

Location in the orchestra:
trombones and tubas

The tuba is a relatively new addition to the brass family and is also the deepest-pitched brass instrument regularly heard in the orchestra.

Like the stringed double bass, the tuba has a reputation for providing valuable support to other instruments while not being able to do much on its own. However, Vaughan Williams wrote a concerto for it.

DID YOU KNOW?

the gigantic brass sousaphone, invented by John Philip Sousa in 1910, stands over 7 ft (2m) high.

▼ The tuba has piston valves similar to those of the trumpet and horn.

Third valve

Second valve

First valve

Mouthpiece

Piston valve

Water key

Wagner tubas are named after the composer Richard Wagner, who developed them for use in his epic cycle of operas, *The Ring of the Nibelungs*. The Austrian composer Anton Bruckner introduced them into the symphony orchestra.

THE ORGAN

Some people think of the organ only in connection with churches and hymns. But the organ has a very long and colorful history. Much great music has been written for it, and it has played a part in the story of the orchestra.

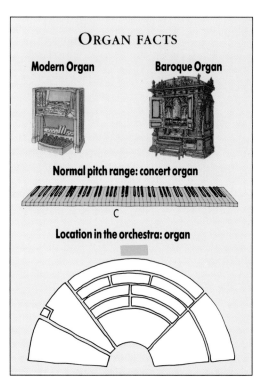

ORGAN FACTS

Modern Organ **Baroque Organ**

Normal pitch range: concert organ

C

Location in the orchestra: organ

▶ The magnificent organ in the Royal Albert Hall, in London, England, was designed for grand ceremonial occasions.

DID YOU KNOW?

the loudest musical instrument ever built, the Auditorium Organ in Atlantic City, New Jersey, makes as much noise as 25 brass bands.

▼ A modern organ console, with three manuals (keyboards), has a pedal keyboard and drawstops for selecting groups of pipes.

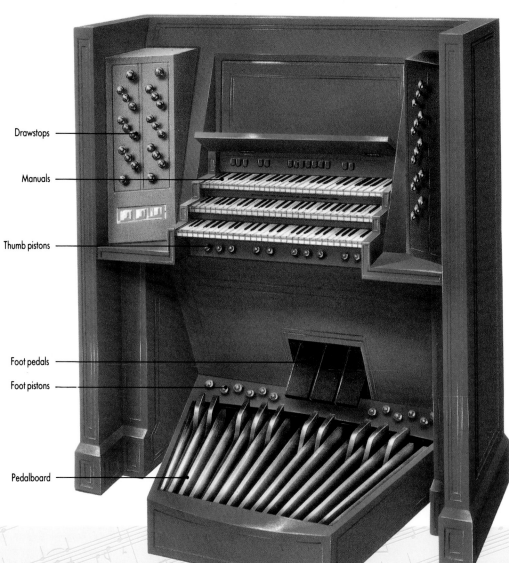

Drawstops

Manuals

Thumb pistons

Foot pedals

Foot pistons

Pedalboard

LISTEN FOR:

ORGAN
. . . .

Saint-Saens:
Symphony No. 3,
"*Organ* symphony"
(especially the last
movement)

Richard Strauss:
Symphonic poem, *Also
Sprach Zarathustra*

Vaughan Williams:
Ballet, *Job*

The organ is a wind instrument, in which air is blown mechanically into a range of pipes of different pitch and tone. It also has keyboards. Some of these look exactly like the one on a piano. Others are more like a set of pedals. Playing on these, with hands and feet, directs air into the pipes.

One of the earliest types of organ, going back two thousand years, was the Greek-named hydraulus, or water organ, which used water pressure to force air through a small set of pipes. In the Middle Ages and Renaissance periods, some large instruments were built with huge sets of bellows to pump air into the pipes. At the other end of the scale, there were small portable types, which were popular entertainment for the rich.

In Bach's and Handel's time, organ builders, such as the German brothers Andreas and Gottfried Silbermann, made some of the most beautiful instruments, often richly decorated with wood carving and gilt. Instruments like this, installed in churches and large halls, sometimes joined in orchestral music.

In the nineteenth century, other organ builders, notably the Frenchman Aristide Cavaillé-Col, made gigantic instruments for churches, town halls, and concert halls. It was during this time that Liszt, Saint-Saëns, and other composers started adding the organ to the orchestra when they wanted a majestic sound.

Modern concert organs are generally smaller in size, and composers continue to include them in orchestral pieces. They have sometimes also written optional organ parts.

▼ The famous Compenius organ stands in Fredericksborg Castle, Denmark. Built around 1615, it is a fine example of baroque organ building.

67

THE PERCUSSION

Percussion describes instruments that are struck or that strike themselves in some way. However, some instruments included as percussion are not actually played like this. The first division falls between membranophones and idiophones. Percussion instruments may also be divided between instruments of "definite pitch" and "indefinite pitch." They form the most varied group of orchestra instruments, from drums to xylophones, bells, gongs, cymbals, wood blocks, and many others. In the concert hall, ranged behind the rest of the orchestra, the percussion instruments are always the main focus of interest and attention. In performance they add much to the variety, color, and sparkle of orchestral sound.

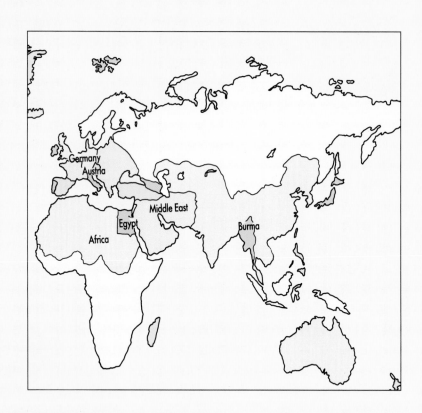

▼ Arabic *naqara* could be tuned by inserting sticks into the lacing to tighten the skin.

▲ Kettledrums were originally used by army musicians. This kettledrum dates from about 1770.

▼ Modern timpani are tuned using the keys around the edge. The pitch of the sound can be altered using the foot pedal.

▲ Xylophone (Sierra Leone), with wooden bars and gourd resonators beneath.

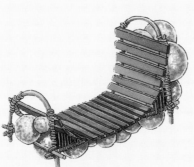

▲ African xylophone.

▲ The tambourine originated in the Middle East. This one has metal jingles, and comes from Spain.

▼ Gongs originated in China. This gong produces a note of indefinite pitch.

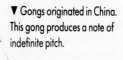

◀ Gong that is tuned to produce a particular note.

▲ An ancient Egyptian systrum – a type of rattle used for religious rituals.

▶ Burmese gong strung between statues of mythological figures.

◀ A nineteenth-century side drum, often carried at the side of the body and played by soldiers on the march.

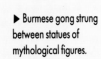

▶ This Turkish waisted drum is played either with the hands or with sticks.

The snare drum is a descendant of the military side drum (below). The snare drum has two skins. The lower skin has a metal or gut wire strung across it (called the snare) so that when the upper skin is struck, the wire vibrates to give the characteristic rattling sound.

▼ This tabla is a form of drum used in India.

▲ Cedarwood rattle from Colombia.

▲ Familiar Spanish castanets, played in one hand, often to accompany traditional Spanish dancing.

69

HOW PERCUSSION INSTRUMENTS WORK

Membranophones include drums. As the word suggests, these are made from some kind of membrane, traditionally an animal skin or hide. This is stretched over a resonating frame, usually enclosed like a pot, or enclosed by having a membrane stretched across it at both ends. When the drummer strikes the skin, with sticks or with his own hands and fingers, it vibrates, and both the frame and the air inside it take up the vibrations and give them volume and tone. This is the basis of African tribal drums, the smaller, hand-beaten tabla drums of India, the

military drums used on the parade ground, and the large timpani or kettledrums heard in the orchestra.

The same acoustic principles apply to membranophones as to stringed instruments. The tighter the membrane, the faster it will vibrate when struck, and the higher will be the sound. Size also has much to do with a drum's pitch and tone. A drum with a large area of membrane and a correspondingly large resonating frame will sound much deeper and more full-bodied than a small one.

Some drums are percussion instruments of definite pitch. Depending on the tautness of their

▲ Some instruments, such as cymbals and triangles have indefinite pitch. This means that while you can tell whether the tone produced is high or low, it is difficult to tell exactly which note of the scale is sounding.

BANGING THE DRUM

It is possible to play percussion instruments in many ways. All drums can be played without sticks. This produces a short, dull sound. Skilled drummers (1) can produce a wide variety of sounds with their hands. The bass drum is usually played with a soft stick (2), producing a low, resonant sound. Sometimes, the player "stops" the sound from going on too long by touching the drumhead with a hand. The tenor drum (3) is most often played with hard sticks to produce a short, sharp sound. The side drum (4) can also be played using hard sticks, but wire brushes produce a more unusual effect. Drawn across the drumhead, the drum's snares rattle quietly to produce a sound like the sea on a pebbly beach.

1

2

3

4

MAKING SOUNDS WITH DRUMS

The length, volume, and pitch of the sound made by a drum depends on its size and the tightness of the skin (drumhead). When the drum is struck, it vibrates, and these vibrations travel across the drumhead and through its sides. The air inside the drum also vibrates, increasing the volume of the sound. The larger the drum, the louder the noise!

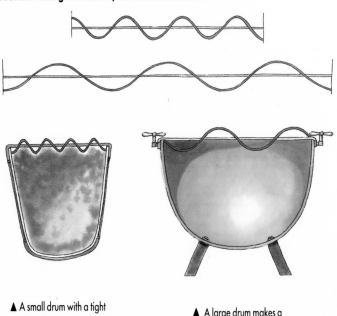

▲ A small drum with a tight drumhead makes a dull, high-pitched sound which lasts only a short time.

▲ A large drum makes a generally lower-pitched note, which can resonate for much longer.

Orchestral kettledrums have a definite pitch. The drum's pedal allows the player to change the tightness of the skin, and so the pitch of the note, quickly and easily. Pressing the pedal pulls on the drum's rim, which in turn tightens the drumhead to produce a higher note.

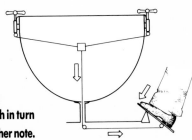

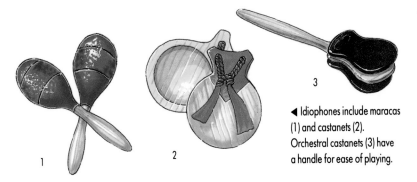

◄ Idiophones include maracas (1) and castanets (2). Orchestral castanets (3) have a handle for ease of playing.

skin or drumhead, you can tell the actual pitch of the note they are sounding.

The other large group of percussion instruments are the idiophones. This is another Greek word, meaning "own sound." It describes those instruments made from a single piece of material (stone, wood, bone, or metal). In other words, the material itself vibrates and makes a sound. Knocking two pebbles together is a do-it-yourself idiophone.

An amazing variety of percussion instruments, producing an equally amazing range of crashes, bangs, chimes, thumps, knocks, rattles, and rasps, belong to the category of idiophone. Some of these may be scraped or sounded in some other way than actually being struck. Well-known idiophones include cymbals, gongs, xylophones, and bells. Also included are instruments associated with special kinds of music, such as the castanets of Spanish flamenco song and dance (two cup-shaped pieces of wood or ivory rapped with the fingers) and some percussion instruments from Latin America, such as the maracas (a type of rattle).

Once again, the size of the instrument has much to do with the general pitch and tone of its sound. Compare the deep, resonating chime of a large bell weighing several tons with the jingle of tiny bells worn round the wrists or ankles in some folk songs and dances.

Most bells are instruments of definite pitch. Cymbals and gongs, on the other hand, are of indefinite pitch. You can only guess at their degree of highness or lowness through the clash or resonating hum of all their vibrations.

DRUMS

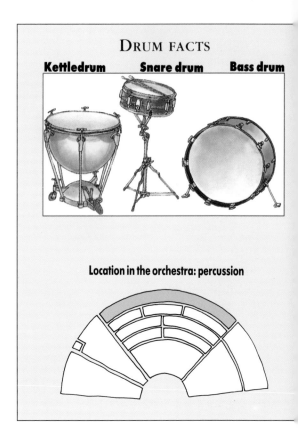

DRUM FACTS

Kettledrum   Snare drum   Bass drum

Location in the orchestra: percussion

The Italian word *timpano* (*timpani* for more than one) is now the most widely used word for the kettledrum. With tight skins stretched over a large metal resonating bowl, they are the classic orchestral drum. The timpanist sits at the back of the platform, usually above the brass.

The timpani probably came to Europe from the Middle East during the Crusades (the twelfth and thirteenth centuries), and had a ceremonial and military use. They are instruments of definite pitch, their note being determined by how tightly the skin or drumhead is stretched.

Up to the time of Beethoven, an orchestra usually had two timpani,

▼ The timpanist usually sits or stands high up at the back of the orchestra, like the king of the castle.

tuned to the basic notes of the key in which the music was written. If the music changed key, the timpani had to remain silent, since it was not possible to retune them. They were played with wooden drumsticks, rather than the padded sticks that are used today.

Since Beethoven's time, composers have added as many as six timpani to the orchestra, needing two timpanists to play them. In the early years of this century came pedal-operated instruments, giving composers even greater opportunities.

The timpani can sound like musical thunder. They beat out a rhythm with solid strength, carrying the music along with them. They also play drum rolls (rapidly repeated notes), and they may be muffled by placing a cloth over the drumhead, or extra padding on the sticks.

The side and bass drums are of indefinite pitch. The pitch of their sound is difficult to judge, although the tone of the side drum is clearly much higher than that of the bass drum.

The side or snare drum is close in sound to military drums that beat out a rhythm for marching soldiers. It has two drumheads, one often fitted with a set of wires called snares, to give a brisker sound. The drummer can also make "rim-shots," slapping the stick across the rim and head of the drum to create a crack like a gun shot.

▶ Drumsticks used include (from top to bottom): wire brushes sometimes used on side drums and cymbals; traditional hard sticks; and padded sticks for timpani and bass drum.

LISTEN FOR:

TIMPANI

Haydn:
Symphony No. 103 "Drum Roll" heard at the start

Beethoven:
Symphony No. 9, "Choral" (especially the sudden three-note motifs in the second movement)

Richard Strauss:
Symphonic poem, *Also Sprach Zarathustra* (opening bars)

SIDE DRUM

Richard Strauss:
Symphonic poem, *Till Eulenspiegel* (near the end)

Ravel:
Bolero

BASS DRUM

Beethoven:
Symphony No. 9, "Choral" (march section of last movement)

Borodin:
"Polovtsian Dances" from opera *Prince Igor* (third dance)

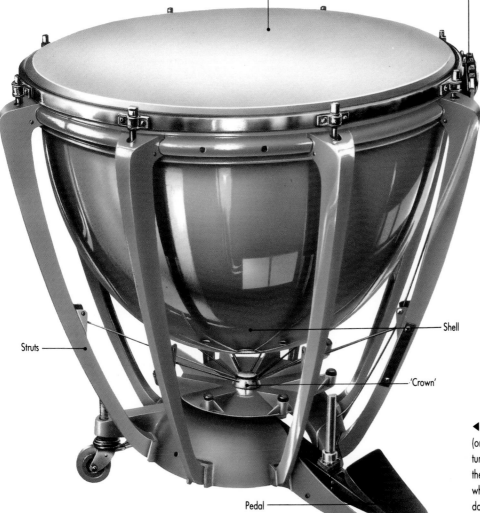

Drum head

Tuning gauge

Shell

Struts

'Crown'

Pedal

◀ The modern kettledrum (or timpano) has a pedal for tuning. The timpanist can use the pedal to change the note while playing, to glide up and down between two notes.

OTHER PERCUSSION

▼ Tubular bells are metal tubes of different lengths, suspended from a frame.

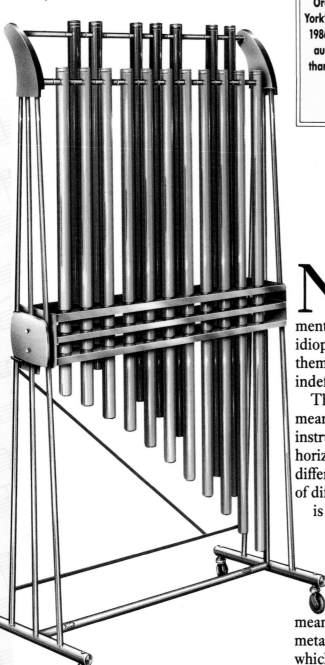

DID YOU KNOW?

a concert by the New York Philharmonic Orchestra in New York's Central Park in 1986, drew a record audience of more than 80,000 people.

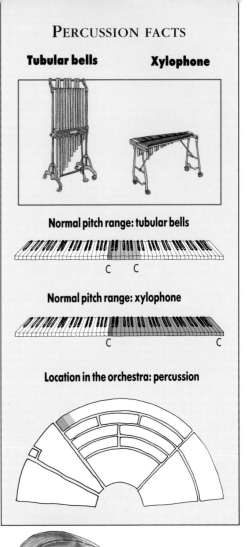

PERCUSSION FACTS

Tubular bells   **Xylophone**

Normal pitch range: tubular bells

C   C

Normal pitch range: xylophone

C   C

Location in the orchestra: percussion

◀ Cymbals (left) can be crashed together to produce a single, dramatic noise. The Chinese gong, on the other hand is best struck softly but continuously to produce a growing wave of sound.

Nearly all the other percussion instruments of the orchestra are idiophones. It is best to divide them between those of definite and indefinite pitch.

The xylophone (a Greek word meaning "wooden sound") is an instrument of definite pitch, with its horizontally placed wooden bars of different size each tuned to a note of different pitch. The marimba is basically a larger, deeper, and more mellow-sounding type of xylophone.

The glockenspiel (a German name that means "play of bells"), has tuned metal bars instead of wooden ones, which bring it closer in sound to

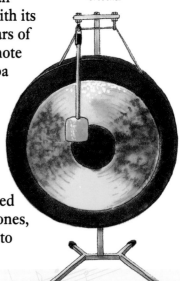

the tinkle of bells. Tubular bells or chimes, metal tubes of different length, are struck with hammers.

▲ The glockenspiel has metal bars set out in the same pattern as the piano.

An interesting cross between the xylophone and glockenspiel is the vibraphone, with steel bars and metal resonators, equipped with small electric fans that add to the vibrating effect, creating soft, pulsating tones.

Gongs or tam-tams, probably originating in China, are sheets of copper, bronze, or other metals beaten into a kind of plate or dish, suspended from a frame and struck with a padded stick or mallet. Made in many different sizes, they can create tremendous vibrations. Cymbals are similar to gongs, but their metalwork, generally, is finer, and they produce a higher-pitched and thrilling clash. Large cymbals may be hand-held and clashed together. Smaller ones are often supported on a stand and struck with various types of drumsticks. The triangle's tinkling note adds a delicate point of sound to the orchestra.

Finally, other "percussion" instruments include the tambourine, wood blocks, clappers, rattles, castanets, cow bells, anvils, sirens, whistles, taxi horns (in Gershwin's *An American in Paris*), rattling iron chains (in Arnold Schoenberg's *Gurrelieder*), and a typewriter (in Erik Satie's *Parade*). They all find their way into what is sometimes jokingly called "the kitchen sink department."

THE WIND MACHINE

The wind machine is another orchestral device classed as percussional, although it is really nothing of the sort. It is a type of revolving barrel inside a tight canvas cover, which creates the sound effect of wind, from a sigh almost to a shriek, depending on how fast the player turns the handle of the barrel. Listen for it in Ravel's ballet music to *Daphnis and Chloe* and Vaughan Williams's *Sinfonia Antarctica*.

▼ The xylophone's wooden bars are struck with hard sticks, often at very high speed.

LISTEN FOR:

XYLOPHONE

Saint-Saëns:
The Carnival of the Animals ("Fossils")

Holst:
The Planets ("Uranus")

TUBULAR BELLS, TAMBOURINE, AND CASTANETS

Debussy:
"Iberia" from *Images*

GONG

Gershwin:
Piano Concerto in F (toward the end of the last movement)

CYMBALS

Bizet:
Prelude to the opera *Carmen*

Tchaikovsky:
Fantasy-overture *Romeo and Juliet*

TRIANGLE

Liszt:
Piano Concerto No. 1 (second part of second movement)

75

ELECTRONIC INSTRUMENTS

Electrically aided instruments are conventional instruments such as the violin, piano, and guitar, which are wired up for sound. True electronic instruments generate their own sounds in the first place.

An American inventor, Thaddeus Cahill, was a pioneer in the field of electronic instruments. In 1906 he built his telharmonium, but this was so huge and heavy that nobody could make much use of it. Another American, Lee de Forest, perfected the valve oscillator, a piece of electronics that converted electrical impulses or signals into sound waves. Valve oscillators, photo-electric cells, and other scientific discoveries soon became the basis for the first real generation of electronic instruments, including the well-known Hammond organ, created by the American Laurens Hammond. Coming closer to the present day, two more American inventors, Robert Moog and Donald Buchla, produced the first electronic synthesizer. This amazing invention generated its own sound impulses and synthesized them — built them up — into a whole new body of sound. A synthesizer can reproduce the sound of any existing instrument, or create an almost unlimited range of new sounds.

The tape recorder, another electronic device, has also been used to create a new world of sound. Soon after its invention, during World War II, composers began to experiment with tapes. They recorded all sorts of everyday sounds (trains, cars, people

▲ The modern synthesizer has many keyboards. It is used to reproduce the sounds of known instruments and to create entirely new sounds.

WRITING IT DOWN

Some modern composers make use of many different recorded noises and electronic instruments. Composers found that it was impossible to write down the kinds of things they wanted using a traditional musical score, so they created their own form of "graphic" musical notation. This graphic score is from Cornelius Cardew's piece *Treatise*, which was composed in 1967.

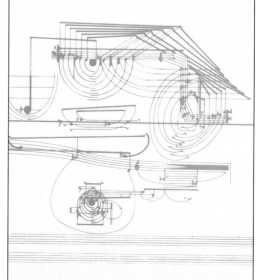

talking), as well as musical ones, then rerecorded them speeded up, slowed down, played backwards, or cut up and reassembled. Composers called their work with tape recorders *musique concrète*, that is, music or sound effects created from basic, everyday sounds.

The orchestra stood on the sidelines while much of this work was going on. Indeed, some composers, fascinated by the new possibilities opened up by tapes and synthesizers (and more recently still, by computers) have turned their backs on the orchestra entirely. Others, however, have been interested in finding out how the sounds of the orchestra and of electronic instruments could work together.

The French-Swiss composer Honneger was one of the first to include, in his oratorio *Joan of Arc at the Stake*, the electronic Ondes Martenot ("Martenot Waves"). Named after its inventor, the Frenchman Maurice Martenot, it sounds a single note, which can drift up and down in pitch, in a strange, pure tone. More recently, the French composer Olivier Messiaen, also very interested in religious and mystical experiences, made even more use of the Ondes Martenot in his gigantic *Turangalîla* symphony and other orchestral works.

The German composer Karlheinz Stockhausen, a pioneer of *musique concrète*, has combined prerecorded tapes with an orchestra in some of his works. Milton Babbitt, Luciano Berio, Pierre Boulez, and Roberto Gerhard are other composers who have brought together the sound worlds of the orchestra and electronics.

DID YOU KNOW?

the first piece written specifically for an electric instrument was *First Airphonic Suite*, by Joseph Schillinger in 1929, written for the thérémin.

◀ The traditional violin can be amplified or connected to a synthesizer by attaching a sound pickup, known as a bug, to the instrument. The bug is usually positioned close to the bridge of the instrument because that is the place where it will pickup the most balanced sound. Violins that are modified in this way are most often used in performance of jazz and rock music.

CHAPTER 3

A Day in the Life of the Orchestra

Music is in many ways a far more complex business than writing and reading books, or creating and viewing paintings and sculptures. Most Western music is composed and written down. Then it has to be performed by other people playing a large variety of instruments. All this takes a lot of organizing. A very large orchestra needs a great deal of organization. To start with there are the players (up to a hundred) with their instruments and their music. They lead a busy and hectic life. Then there is all the administration and money that goes into an orchestral performance. It adds up to a major operation.

LIZ OF THE LSO

Elizabeth Greaves joined the London Symphony Orchestra in 1988, as soon as she left music college. She now plays in the first violin section. Liz started learning the violin when she was eight years old. Four years later she joined a youth orchestra, and at that point decided that she wanted to become a violin player in an orchestra. Working in a major orchestra such as the LSO is a very demanding job. However, music is only one of Liz's interests; she also loves gymnastics, water sports, food, wine, and shopping!

▼ Liz on her way to rehearsal. Normally, the LSO starts rehearsing at around 10:00 a.m. The rehearsal lasts for three hours, with a twenty-minute break.

Playing in a big international orchestra is one of life's most exciting experiences. It is also a tough job. Players are part of a team of eighty or more musicians, playing some of the world's greatest music. They work very long hours: turning up early for rehearsals on a dark, cold winter's morning in a chilly, empty hall; working till late in the evening on the night of a concert; traveling on trains and planes at all hours of the day and night; eating and sleeping when they can; trying to play well when they are tired or hungry or have a headache. There's not much time left for home, family, or friends. In fact, their "family" is the rest of the orchestra. The musicians share the hectic pace and the worries. But they also share the wonderful moments when they are all playing well together and feel on top of the world. That makes it all worthwhile.

Rehearsals

Much of an orchestra's time is spent in rehearsal. The players may already know the music by heart. But every conductor has his own ideas about how a piece of music should be played. That's one reason why rehearsals are necessary. Another reason is the problem of orchestral balance of sound. With the rest of the orchestra around them, players cannot always hear themselves properly (sometimes not at all), and so they cannot gauge the balance of sound between their own instruments or section, and the rest of the orchestra. At rehearsals this is something that the conductor is able to put right.

Some conductors like to go through a piece of music bar by bar, stopping the orchestra each time they want to make a comment. Others let the orchestra play for long stretches at a time, then go back to a particular point they want to rehearse again.

Whatever the conductor's method, it is important that the musicians are happy with it. If the players don't like the conductor they can become very difficult, interrupting the session with questions or complaints. At one time, conductors such as Toscanini used to get fine performances out of an orchestra by shouting at the musicians, almost frightening them into playing well. That sort of behavior would not work with most orchestras today. After all, orchestral musicians are highly trained and experienced people, and they should be treated with respect.

◀ Warming up before the rehearsal starts. Liz also practices at home for up to twenty hours a week.

▼ Michael Tilson Thomas, the LSO's principal conductor, raises his baton to start the rehearsal.

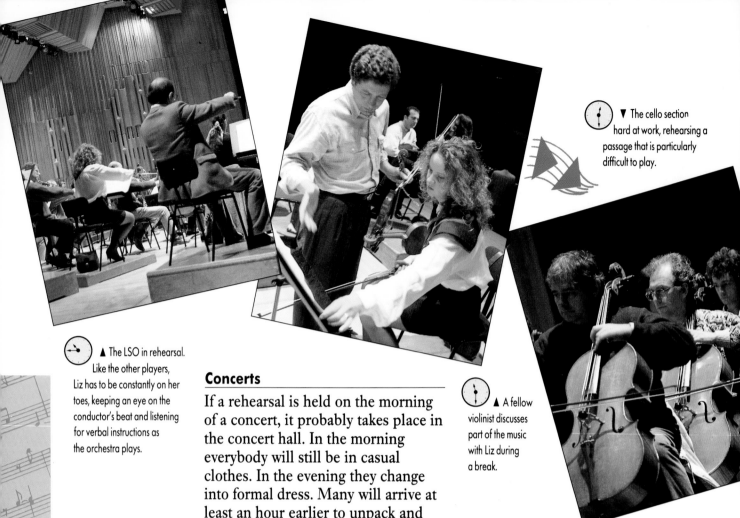

▼ The cello section hard at work, rehearsing a passage that is particularly difficult to play.

▲ The LSO in rehearsal. Like the other players, Liz has to be constantly on her toes, keeping an eye on the conductor's beat and listening for verbal instructions as the orchestra plays.

▲ A fellow violinist discusses part of the music with Liz during a break.

Concerts

If a rehearsal is held on the morning of a concert, it probably takes place in the concert hall. In the morning everybody will still be in casual clothes. In the evening they change into formal dress. Many will arrive at least an hour earlier to unpack and inspect their instruments – violinists to check their strings and bow, woodwind players to check their reeds and change them if necessary – and also to run over any difficult passages of the music. If they want a bit of peace and quiet they may even hide themselves away in the rest rooms or creep down to the boiler room! Players whose instruments are too big for them to carry – timpani, harps, double basses – will arrive on the platform before the rest, making the same last-minute checks.

About five minutes before the concert is due to start, everybody, except the leader or concert master, files on and takes their place. Then the leader comes on, to a round of applause from the audience, and calls for silence, while the oboist sounds the note A. The rest of the orchestra tune their instruments to this note.

Finally, on comes the conductor, to more applause. When there is quiet once more, the concert can begin.

However well the orchestra may have rehearsed, there can still be problems for them. In a warm, crowded concert hall, the acoustics are different from those in a cool, empty building, and this can change the balance of orchestral sound. Also, instruments may go out of tune after a little while in a warm atmosphere.

Musicians, like actors, are also aware of the audience. They notice whether the audience is a good one, which listens and responds to the music, or whether the audience coughs and fidgets throughout the performance. Above all, the musicians know whether they are playing well, not just individually but

After three hard hours, the orchestra breaks for lunch. If an afternoon rehearsal is called it will also last three hours, from 2 p.m. to 5 p.m.

as a team. Knowing that they're giving a good performance makes all the difference at the end of a long, hard day.

Recordings

On days when they are not rehearsing, giving a concert, or traveling from one place to another, an orchestra is probably making a recording or doing film and television work. Some players don't enjoy this very much. They miss the audience and the excitement of a live concert. In a recording or television studio, they find it difficult to put their heart into their performance. But recordings and film music pay well, so they are often glad to have the work.

Recording today depends as much on the electronics engineers and technicians as on the orchestra and conductor. They decide where the musicians should sit, often separating them from each other by acoustic panels so that the various microphones only pick up their particular sounds. It is up to the engineers in the control room to

WHAT MAKES A GOOD CONCERT HALL

How good an orchestra sounds does not depend solely on the skill of its players, it also depends on where they are playing. In some old concert halls, for instance, sound bounces off walls and the ceiling in a way that makes the music sound sharp and edgy. In others, the music can echo around the building, so that it is difficult to hear it clearly. If sound echoes around a concert hall, it is called a "live" hall. A hall in which the sound does not resonate enough is said to be "dead." When a new concert hall is being built, experts in the science of sound (which is called acoustics) are asked to advise the architects. They always aim to build a hall that is neither too "live" nor too "dead."

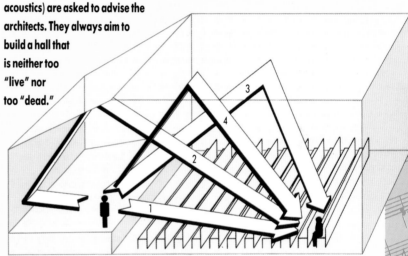

▲ The sounds made by musicians on the stage of a concert hall reach the listener by four basic paths: (1) the direct path, reaching the listener before it reaches any other surfaces; (2) the path reflected off the stage; (3) the path reflected from the walls; and the path reflected from the ceiling (4). As you will see, each of these paths is a different length, so it takes the sound on each of the paths a slightly different amount of time to reach the listener.

When building a concert hall, it is the job of the acoustics expert to make sure that the time delays between the sounds reaching the listener by each of the paths are not too long.

▶ Sydney Opera House, Australia, was opened in 1973. It has a concert hall, an opera auditorium, a theater, a movie theater, and a recital room, as well as a sound recording studio and rehearsal rooms.

On the evening of the concert, musicians check their instruments, then leave their cases in a back room.

Liz makes up before the concert. Evening dress is the rule – the men wear white ties and tails; the women wear black dresses.

blend or mix the individual instruments into the sound of the whole orchestra.

At the start of a session, the conductor usually leads the orchestra through a section of the music, while the engineers check all their equipment for sound. Then they start the actual recording. The "hot line" telephone by the conductor's side may ring. "Sorry," says one of the engineers from the control room, "there's been a technical hitch. You'll have to start again." They do. One of the players may fluff a note. They have to go back and correct the mistake.

At the end of the take, the conductor, and perhaps the leader of the orchestra and section principals,

IT'S A GREAT LIFE

Touring is one of the bonuses of being a member of a modern orchestra such as the LSO. Liz has traveled with the LSO to North America, Australia, Japan, and throughout Europe, playing in Paris, Berlin, and at the Salzburg Festival. The LSO has been visiting Daytona Beach, Florida, since 1966. The first trip involved transporting ninety-six players, forty-three wives, and thirty-six children, plus two tons of instruments and enough scores for two full concerts a week, plus additional chamber concerts, over a month. Despite a hectic work schedule, members of the orchestra always find time to enjoy themselves, as this picture of the horn section posing in a Daytona Beach hotel pool shows.

Now the long hours of rehearsal prove their worth, as Michael Tilson Thomas leads the LSO in performance.

After the concert, Liz and violin say good night and go off to meet some friends.

go into the control room to listen to the recording. The rest of the orchestra sit and wait. If anyone is still unhappy with a part of the recording, the musicians play that passage again. It continues until everyone is happy.

Television and Motion Picture work

Recording a musical sound track for a movie, television program, or commercial is a tricky operation. First the composer must write music that fits each sequence of the film or commercial. On the day of the recording the conductor must make sure the composition works. He watches a playback of the film on a large screen as he directs the orchestra and uses indications in the score to judge the right tempo or pace of the music for the action on the screen. If the music ends too early or too late for the sequence, even by a second or two, he and his orchestra must do it again. Work like this demands a good deal of patience as well as skill.

Auditions

There is a constant turnover among the players of an orchestra. Some of the older ones retire. Some move on to other work. That means that the orchestra is always looking for promising new musicians. At the same time, there is plenty of competition among young and ambitious musicians to join a big orchestra, despite the tough life we have described. So the orchestra holds regular auditions.

These auditions are a cross between an examination and a job interview. The orchestra's chief conductor, section principals, and perhaps one or two experienced music teachers or other players from outside the orchestra sit on one side. On the other side are the candidates. Most of these will have studied for three or four years at a musical academy or college and will have good technical qualifications. Some may already have experience.

As with other exams and job interviews, there are right and wrong ways of going about auditions. The adjudicators don't like show-offs. Nor do they like people who look sloppy or turn up late. They are not only looking for expert players, but also for people who will fit into the communal life of an orchestra. The orchestra, after all, will become their family.

85

Running an Orchestra

An orchestra is also a business, with a great deal of organization and administration behind it. Some orchestras, such as the BBC Symphony Orchestra in London, and the orchestras of opera houses, are part of larger organizations. Others exist on their own. They control their own affairs, with a board of directors or a management committee often elected by the players themselves. This board or committee then appoints such important people as a chief conductor and a general manager.

Program Planning

When we see an orchestra in the concert hall, or hear one of its recordings on a CD or cassette, what we are seeing or hearing was all arranged months, or even years, beforehand. An orchestra's management is always planning ahead.

Planning the concert programs entails a lot of hard work. Some orchestras specialize in music of a

◄ A moving van is used to take the larger instruments to a recording studio.

▼ In the studio, microphone booms crowd around the conductor and the players. The conductor is wearing headphones, so, in this movie-music recording, he can listen to the soundtrack and cue the orchestra accordingly.

RECORDING WITH THE ORCHESTRA

▼ In the control booth. The two recording engineers in the foreground mix the sound; you can see the controls they use to do this on the console in front of them. The producer, the person in charge, is sitting at the table behind the engineers, following what is going on in his copy of the score.

▼ When the music is being recorded, absolute quiet is essential – the microphones will pick up any unwanted noise, such as a dropped bow or a whispered word.

School orchestras provide young players with an opportunity to be part of a musical team (right) – many players in the world's top orchestras started their careers in just this way. You may be lucky enough to go to a school that professional musicians sometimes visit to entertain and instruct (below). This little boy (far right) has been given a rare opportunity to indulge his dream – conducting a famous orchestra. Stick with your instrument and keep practicing.

particular period or style, which may make their job a little easier. But a big international orchestra must include in its repertory and programs the music of many composers, periods, and styles. It does not want to bore its audience with the same popular classics each time. On the other hand, it must not frighten people with music that is too new and unfamiliar.

Deciding on the program itself is only half the battle. The orchestra must also engage soloists, other conductors besides their own resident or chief conductor (who will have engagements elsewhere), and perhaps extra players for large-scale works. Some orchestras have their own choir or chorus. Others may have to book a choir and other vocalists for choral works.

The Librarian

We think of librarians as quiet people. But the life of an orchestral librarian can be hectic. He or she looks after the orchestra's music. For an orchestra, every piece of music has to be broken down into parts for each player – that means between forty and a hundred or more individual parts of printed music for each composition. The librarian sees that all the parts of a work (plus a full score for the conductor) are ready and waiting on everybody's music stand before a rehearsal or concert.

The librarian must have a very good technical knowledge of music. Orchestral parts are not usually printed with such markings as fingerings, or in the case of the strings, bowing marks (indications of how to draw the bow up and down across the strings). So, where possible, the librarian puts these marks in for each part. At rehearsal, however, a conductor may get the players to change some of the markings. Afterward, the librarian must decide whether or not to leave these changes as they are. Orchestral parts would soon become a mess of penciled-in and crossed-out marks if the librarian did not keep them neat.

> **DID YOU KNOW?**
>
> conductor Herbert von Karajan (1908–89) made over 800 orchestral recordings – more than any other conductor.

87

GLOSSARY

A

Arpeggio The notes of a chord (three or more notes) played one after the other instead of together, as on a harp.

Arrangement An adaptation of a piece of music to be played by a particular combination of instruments and voices.

B

Bar A measure or length of music as it is read or played.

Baroque Style or period of music from about 1600 to 1750, which mixed stately and lively melodies.

C

Clarino trumpet High, clear style of trumpet playing, popular in baroque music.

Classical An orderly style of music from about 1750 to 1800, usually featuring a single melody.

Concerto Compositions for one or more solo instruments and orchestra, usually in three separate sections, or "movements."

Concerto grosso The term means "great concerto," or a type of baroque composition for string orchestra in which a large group of players is contrasted with a much smaller group, or a soloist.

Continuo A special music part for organ or harpsichord in many baroque compositions, used to guide the other players.

Crook Extra length of tubing that can be added to old horns and trumpets to change the range of their notes.

D

Dynamics The contrasts between soft and loud in a piece of music.

E

Embouchure French word for the mouthpiece of wind instruments, also the method of blowing into them.

G

Glissando Italian word meaning "slide;" literally sliding up and down a series of notes very rapidly.

I

Incidental music Music written to accompany a play; motion picture and television music are also kinds of incidental music.

N

Notation Any system of writing down music.

O

Opera Italian word meaning "works;" a play set to music, for singers and orchestra.

Oratorio Special type of opera, usually with a religious story, often performed in a church or concert hall instead of a theater.

Overture From the French word for "opening;" music played at the beginning of an opera, ballet, or play. A "concert overture" is a piece on its own, written specially for concerts.

P

Pitch The highness or lowness of a musical note.

Pizzicato Italian for "pinched;" instruction to string players to pluck the strings of their instruments, rather than bow them.

Polyphony Meaning "many sounds;" style of music using one or more melodies repeated many times, often woven together, much used by Renaissance and baroque composers.

Program music Music that describes a story, place, or event, or evokes special feelings or ideas.

R

Recitative Sung dialogue accompanied by the continuo in classical operas.

Renaissance Style or period of music from about 1400 to 1600.

Rhythm The basic beat of a piece of music, counted as so many beats to the bar.

Romantic Style or period of music from about 1800 to 1900; an imaginative style that is often a loving reminder of nature.

S

Scherzo Literally a "joke," but more generally a fairly fast and dramatic piece of music.

Score A written piece of music showing how all the vocal and instrumental parts should be played.

Sinfonia Old Italian word for symphony, originally a kind of overture.

Soloist A musician playing or singing a solo part.

Stopping Depressing the string of a stringed instrument to alter its playing length and the pitch of its note.

Suite From the French word meaning "following" or "succession;" composition consisting of a series of pieces, usually elegant dances. Can also describe a selection of music taken from a larger composition.

Symphonic poem Piece of music usually inspired by a story, poem, or picture.

Symphony Usually a large-scale orchestral composition and normally consisting of four separate pieces of music, or "movements." Some symphonies include voices.

T

Tempo The speed or pace of a piece of music, as distinct from its rhythm.

Tremolo Italian for "shaking;" rapid drawing of a bow back and forth across a string to create a shuddering effect.

Tutti Italian for "all;" often used in concertos to describe passages where the orchestra plays without a soloist.

Other well known musical terms:
The following terms are written on musical scores to show how a composer wants the music, or certain parts of it, to be played.

A Tempo Keep to the speed, or return to original speed.

Accelerando Accelerate; gradually increase the speed.

Adagio Fairly slow; **adagio maestoso,** slow and majestic, or grand.

Allegro Fairly fast; **allegro ma non troppo,** not too fast; **allegro con brio,** quite fast and spirited.

Andante At a leisurely pace; **andante cantabile,** leisurely and in a singing style.

Bravura A spirited, brilliant style of playing.

Coda Tailpiece, concluding section of a piece of music.

Crescendo (cresc) Play gradually louder.

Da Capo (D.C.) Go back to the beginning.

Forte (f) Loud; **fortissimo (ff),** very loud.

Largo Slow and stately.

Legato Play smoothly, flowingly.

Lento Slow.

Piano (p) Soft or quiet; **pianissimo (pp),** very soft or quiet.

Presto Fast; **prestissimo,** very fast.

Rallentando (rall) Gradually slow down; **ritardando (rit)** means almost the same thing.

Rubato Play with some fluctuations of tempo.

Sforzando Play a chord or note very strongly, forcefully.

Staccato Play in a very detached, precise way.

Vivace Lively, bright.

INDEX

ACKNOWLEDGEMENTS

Picture Credits

Bildarchiv Preussischer Kulturbesitz 21b; ET Archive 14bl, 15b, 15al, 17cr, 20cr, 23ar, 25ar, 27ac, 27bc, 28cl, 30ac, 32c; Chris Christodoulou 67al; Hulton Deutsch Picture Company 17ar, 33ar; London Symphony Orchestra 36, 37; The Mansell Collection 16cr, 17c, 26cl, 32ac, David Redfern 10, 11.

While every effort has been made to trace and acknowledge all copyright holders, we would like to apologize should any omissions have been made.